COMMUNICATION
ETHICS
METHODS OF
ANALYSIS

COMMUNICATION

ETHICS

METHODS OF

A·N·A·L·Y·S·I·S

JAMES A. JAKSA

MICHAEL S. PRITCHARD

Western Michigan University

Wadsworth Publishing Company
Belmont, California
A Division of Wadsworth, Inc.

Communications Editor: *Kristine M. Clerkin*
Production Editor: *Leland Moss*
Editorial Assistant: *Melissa Harris*
Managing Designer: *Donna Davis*
Designer: *John Osborne*
Print Buyer: *Barbara Britton*
Copy Editor: *Anne Montague*
Compositor: *DEKR*
Cover: *Donna Davis*
Signing Representative: *Don Fehr*

Printed in the United States of America   **49**

1 2 3 4 5 6 7 8 9 10—92 91 90 89 88

Library of Congress Cataloging-in-Publication Data

Jaksa, James A., 1931–
  Communication ethics.

  Bibliography: p.
  Includes index.
  1. Ethics. 2. Social ethics. 3. Communication—
Moral and ethical aspects. I. Pritchard, Michael S.
II. Title.
BJ1012.J36 1988   170   87-31583
ISBN 0-534-09102-4

CONTENTS

PREFACE

In recent years much public attention has been focused on ethics. For many, mention of ethics in government, business, and the professions immediately suggests a depressingly long list of questionable behavior: Watergate; ABSCAM; the federally supported Tuskegee syphilis study; military experiments with LSD on unsuspecting soldiers; Three Mile Island; Bhopal; exploding Ford Pinto gas tanks; the exposure of unsuspecting asbestos workers to high risk of dangerous, if not fatal, lung disease; the falsification of data by one of Harvard's brightest medical researchers; scandals on Wall Street; and the Iran/Contra controversy.

Important as these events are, taken alone they suggest a misleading picture of ethics. First, ethics is not confined to the newsworthy. After all, relatively few of us, in either our public or private lives, are ever faced with the kinds of momentous situations that attract media attention. Nevertheless, we are faced daily with the need to deal with situations that have ethical dimensions. Second, ethics is not restricted to misconduct. Ethically responsible behavior is possible, perhaps even commonplace.

However, newsworthy ethical concerns—whether about moral scandals or about moral dilemmas resulting from developments in medical technology (for example, kidney machines or life support systems)—have served as a prod for ethical reflection throughout society: Look at the proliferation of conferences, workshops, and courses on ethics. A recent survey indicates that more than 11,000 courses in ethics are being taught at American colleges and universities. Traditionally lodged in departments of philosophy and religion, courses in ethics can now be found in schools of medicine, law, business, and engineering, as well as in a variety of other disciplines, such as psychology, social work, and communication.

This book is written as a response to the growing interest in teaching communication ethics. It is designed to be used either as a textbook for a course in communication ethics or as a supplemental textbook for courses in special areas of communication. We also hope it will be useful for the general reader who is interested in reflecting on typical ethical issues in communication. Although we haven't attempted to be comprehensive, we hope that our approach to ethical issues in communication provides useful models for reflection in virtually all contexts of communication. The authors—one a professor of communication, the other a professor of philosophy—share the view that communication ethics is best studied in an interdisciplinary manner. We have drawn, for example, from the fields of communication, philosophy, moral development, and social psychology. No one discipline seems to us the proper and exclusive home for the study of communication ethics.

In the text, we discuss issues of lying and deception at some length. We are convinced that the topic of lying and deception is fundamental to all areas of communication. It is fundamental in its own right, as a central concern in communication generally. It is also fundamental, we think, in that an examination of the ethical dimensions of lying and deception can provide a model for examining the ethical dimensions of many kinds of nondeceptive communication as well. Rather than try to say something about everything, we have opted for a more in-depth treatment of a smaller range of topics. We hope this decision will enable readers to proceed more effectively on their own into areas of communication ethics that, because of limitations of space and imagination, we have left unexplored.

Readers may be disappointed that we offer no definition of *ethics*. One might think that without such a definition, we cannot find our way. It is true that, without some *understanding* of ethics, we cannot find our way. But all of us do have some understanding of ethics, even if we lack a good definition. We all have ideas about what is, from a moral or ethical perspective, right or wrong, appropriate or inappropriate, decent or indecent, desirable or undesirable, good or bad, and the like. We have ideas about praise, blame, responsibility, irresponsibility, integrity, and moral character. We have been exposed to such ideas since early childhood. We have been judged by others in terms of them, and we have used them in our judgments of others and ourselves. It does not follow, of course, that we all have the same ideas about these matters. And it does not follow that we understand them well, either in themselves or in relation to one another. In fact, it is in part because we are not very clear-headed about much of ethics that studying ethics is important.

If ethics were an unfamiliar subject (like bacteriology, for example), we might need some sort of definition at the outset of our inquiry. We could live our entire lives without ever knowing anything about bacteria (which is not to say that our lives would be unaffected by bacteria). This is not likely in the case of ethics. Ethics, like logic, is a part of our everyday lives. Logic, as a subject for study, takes advantage of the logical abilities already possessed by those who study it. Similarly, ethics as a subject for study takes advantage of the understanding of ethics already possessed by those who study it.

Finally, readers may notice that we shift easily back and forth in our use of *ethics* and *morality*. Neither textbooks nor ordinary language display any clear or consistent patterns of use. Sometimes it may seem more natural to use one term rather than the other, but this is not intended by us to reflect a difference of substance. *Ethics* is frequently associated with codes and might thereby be regarded as a more narrow term than *morality*. But there are moral codes as well as codes of ethics. In philosophy, ethics is usually characterized, more broadly, as the study of morality. But the study of morality is also sometimes referred to as *moral philosophy*.

Acknowledgments

This book is the result of ten years of team-teaching an interdisciplinary course in communication ethics. During those years we have learned much from our students' reactions to what we have presented to them. We have also benefited greatly from the many opportunities we have had to present papers and workshops at conventions of the Speech Communication Association, Central States Speech Association, Southern Speech Communication Association, Western Speech Communication Association, and the Michigan Association of Speech Communication.

We have had the good fortune of working closely with several leading scholars in the field of communication ethics while SCA was establishing its Communication Ethics Commission. We wish to express appreciation to the original officers of the commission: Kenneth Andersen, University of Illinois; Ronald Arnett, Manchester College; J. Vernon Jensen, University of Minnesota; and Richard Johannesen, Northern Illinois University. Their encouragement of our project and the leadership they have provided through their scholarly writings and presentations have been a source of inspiration. We also wish to express appreciation to the many other commission members who have offered us encouragement and advice, most especially: Clifford Christians, University of Illinois; Thomas Cooper, Emerson College; John Ferré, University of Louisville; Karen Greenberg, Franklin Pierce College; Josina Makau, Ohio State University; J. Michael Sproule, Communication

Consultant, Palo Alto, California; Lea Stewart, Rutgers University; and William Todd-Mancillas, California State University at Chico. Finally, we thank Don M. Boileau for keeping us informed of developments in ethics education while he was at the SCA national office.

At our own university, the recent establishment of the Western Michigan University Center for the Study of Ethics in Society further bolstered our project. The center provided us with an interdisciplinary forum for exchanging ideas. One tangible result is our collaboration with Ronald Kramer of WMU's Criminal Justice Program in writing Chapter 9 of this book.

We wish to thank Richard Dieker, chair of WMU's Department of Communication, for supporting our interdisciplinary teaching and writing. Shirley VanHoeven, director of the department's graduate program, was a constant source of support, and she advised many graduate students into taking our course. Graduate students Mary Beauchamp, Tech Seong Chee, Debra Hyatt, and Serena Wolf were especially helpful in some of our research. Peter Northouse and James Gilchrist, directors of the Communication Research Center, publicized our research and provided us with opportunities to discuss our project with colleagues. Steven Rhodes, George Robeck, Jules Rossman, Robert Smith, and Paul Yelsma, all of the Department of Communication, and Joseph Ellin of the Department of Philosophy took a special interest in our work and were very helpful to us.

Michael Pritchard received a professional leave from WMU in the fall of 1985 to work on this book. During this time Indiana University's Poynter Center, directed by David Smith, generously provided him with collegial support as well as comfortable working space and accommodations.

James Jaksa received Assigned Time from his department to do research on various ethics projects related to this book. He thanks his colleagues for their generous support.

George Bohman and Raymond Ross of Wayne State University and Donald Garner of Eastern Illinois are colleagues of James Jaksa who have had a special role over the years in helping him appreciate the importance of ethical communication.

We wish to thank all those at Wadsworth who encouraged and supported the completion of this book. Donald Fehr first pressed us to show him drafts of several chapters. His enthusiasm for our project was instrumental in moving it ahead. It has been a distinct pleasure to work with such a knowledgeable, helpful, and personable editor as Kris Clerkin. Leland Moss, production editor; Peggy Meehan, permissions editor; and other

Wadsworth editors and reviewers provided much constructive advice and helped us stay on schedule.

The Jaksa children, Julie, Catherine, Jeffrey, John, Jennifer, niece Patricia; the Pritchard children, Scott and Susan; and our spouses, Sarah and Millie, cheerfully and understandingly supported our lengthy project— even while they may have doubted that it would ever be completed.

To Sarah
and
Millie

COMMUNICATION
ETHICS
METHODS OF
A·N·A·L·Y·S·I·S

THE NEED
FOR ETHICS

WHY STUDY ETHICS?

For some, the recent flurry of public concern about ethics indicates little more than a temporary fascination with the sordid details of "scandalous" events that have been publicized by the media. In the long run, what can we realistically expect from the proliferation of courses, conferences, and textbooks that have followed the lead of the media? Cynics abound. For example, consider the attitude expressed several years ago in a *Doonesbury* comic strip:

JOAN: Woody, did you see that we're all being required to take a new course in ethics and law?

WOODY: Yeah. I was afraid that was going to happen.

JOAN: You don't think it might be useful?

WOODY: Nah—all that ethics stuff is just more Watergate fallout! Trendy lip service to our better selves.

JOAN: Trendy lip service to our better selves?

WOODY: Absolutely!—I hate to tell you this, Joan. But six months from now moralizing is going to be just another defunct fad!

JOAN: Oh no, I didn't know that.

WOODY: Hey, look—remember the streaking craze?[1]

But Woody seems to have been wrong. Courses in business and professional ethics are still around several years after he made his pronouncement.

Nonetheless, many people may have doubts about the idea of *teaching* ethics. Again, *Doonesbury* is illustrative. A law professor is addressing his ethics class:

PROFESSOR: Let me put it to you all, then—what should a knowledge of the law tempered with a sense of morality produce? (*Silence.*) Why JUSTICE, of course!

STUDENT: Will that be on the exam?

PROFESSOR: Of course not! (*Head slumped into hand while leaning wearily on the rostrum.*)[2]

We might ask students of communication a similar question: "What should a knowledge of different forms of communication tempered with a sense of morality produce?" We would expect the answers to be varied and possibly contentious. But this *Doonesbury* strip suggests that students have the wrong expectations, making us wonder what good might come of ethics courses if students are concerned only with what might appear on an exam. One might even develop the "true skeptic's" attitude—an attitude that could best be articulated by the concepts "Once they're in college it's too late" or "It's fine in theory, but it won't work in practice." A *Mad* magazine cartoon illustrates this attitude well. Two students are walking away from a classroom building:

JOE: I had one hell of a tough "Ethics" exam yesterday!

JANE: I'm not familiar with the subject. What's it about?

JOE: It deals with "philosophical" ethics—Plato, Aristotle, Kant, Dewey! It deals with "Biblical" ethics! It deals with "business" ethics of the marketplace, and it covers "professional" ethics!

JANE: How'd you do on the exam?

JOE (*Glum, with bowed head*): I got an "A."

JANE: That's great! Why aren't you jumping with joy?!

JOE (*Shamefaced*): I cheated![3]

This dialog seems to imply that a connection between theory and practice simply doesn't exist—what we can talk about and reflect on has no bearing on what we do. We may hold out some hope for Joe, however, because he's obviously unhappy with himself—evidence that he has some ethical standards after all.

The Cynical View

But what kinds of standards do people put into practice? Some would say it all depends on who is being judged, a point of view that could be called the "double (or triple) standard." The clearest statement of this view appears in a book on business ethics written more than 50 years ago by two men named (believe it or not) Sharp and Fox:

> So far are business men from being without moral standards that the majority of them, like the majority of other people, have three. There is first the standard which John Smith applies to his treatment of other people—his competitors, his customers, his employees, and those from whom he purchases his supplies. There is, second, the standard which he expects them to apply to him. Finally, there is the standard which he applies to other people's treatment of each other.[4]

This cynical view holds that people will tailor their conception of ethics to serve their own interests—even at the price of consistency. No doubt everyone has some tendency to act this way, albeit perhaps not willfully or deliberately.

Our suggestion is that this cynicism be abandoned in favor of a view expressed by Samuel Florman in his article "Moral Blueprints":

> Skeptics—both within academe and without—argue that moral character is formed in the home, the church, and the community, and cannot be modified in a college classroom or professional symposium. I cannot agree with the skeptics on this count. Most evil acts are committed not by villains but rather by decent human beings—in desperation, momentary weakness, or an inability to discern what is morally right amid the discordant claims of circumstances. The determination to be good may be molded at an early age, but we grapple all our lives with the definition of what is good, or at least acceptable.[5]

If Florman is right, students of ethics need more than moral inspiration. They need to be acquainted with the kinds of circumstances in which they will be called on to engage in moral reflection. They also need opportunities to think through the concepts and principles that are essential to such moral reflection. The neglect of either of these conditions will place students (and those whom their actions affect) at some moral risk.

This problem is nicely illustrated in the early dialogs of Plato. When, in the *Apology*, Socrates says that "the unexamined life is not worth living," he insists on the importance of examining our basic values and the assumptions underlying them.[6] While his assertion may seem unduly severe, we can more modestly suggest that the critical examination of our values can contribute significantly to the quality of our lives. And what is true of value inquiry in general seems equally true of ethical inquiry.

A vivid example of what Socrates has in mind is presented in Plato's *Euthyphro*. Socrates and Euthyphro meet as both are about to go to court.

Socrates is on his way to defend himself against the charge that he believes in false gods and that he has corrupted the youth. Euthyphro is on his way to prosecute someone accused of murder—his own father! Socrates expresses astonishment that Euthyphro would attempt to prosecute his own father, and he asks Euthyphro what his conception of justice is. In the course of their lengthy discussion Euthyphro displays a rather superficial understanding. He complains that Socrates' words seem to be going in a circle, but Socrates replies that he has simply helped Euthyphro work out the implications of his own words—indeed, it is Euthyphro whose thinking is circular. Near the end of the dialog, Socrates asks Euthyphro to try once more to clarify what justice is, but Euthyphro refuses the request: "Another time, then, Socrates. I am in a hurry now, and it is time for me to be off."[7]

Euthyphro, as we have learned, is in a hurry to prosecute his father—in the name of a value whose nature and basis he does not seem to understand. Of course, this situation will not inevitably result in his doing the wrong thing. Perhaps his father is guilty of an injustice that deserves punishment, and perhaps it is not inappropriate for Euthyphro to be the prosecutor. However, Euthyphro is not in a good position to be confident of either. Furthermore, he apparently does not want to take the time to sort these matters out more carefully. The press of circumstances will not permit further delay—the court is about to convene.

Of course, examining one's values does not guarantee that one will always make better decisions than one would make without such reflection. But we can hope that some period of thought will at least increase the odds. Admittedly, classroom reflection on ethical issues is hardly the same as facing real-life problems. But this disparity is more than compensated for by the opportunity students are given to anticipate and reflect on the kinds of ethical issues they are likely to face later. The alternative is the all too common circumstance of having to react rather quickly to a situation one has not anticipated—and perhaps only after some things have already gone wrong.

A Set of Goals

Given all these considerations, what specific objectives can be identified for a course on ethics in communication? The Hastings Center, a pioneer in medical ethics, completed a three-year intensive study of the teaching of applied ethics in higher education. The goals it recommends seem to us quite realistic and sensible. We will discuss four of those goals: (1) stimulating the moral imagination; (2) recognizing ethical issues; (3) developing analytical skills; and (4) tolerating disagreement.[8]

Stimulating the Moral Imagination

Every human action can be seen from a moral point of view; for example, no professional decision is "strictly professional." The Hastings study concludes that without some preparation for meeting moral challenges, the consequences of young professionals' actions may take them by surprise. They may dismiss moral concerns as "unprofessional." This is, according to his own account, precisely what White House counsel John Dean did as he became more and more entangled in the Watergate cover-up.[9] By the time he recognized the extent to which he had compromised his moral judgment, he was caught in a set of moral dilemmas—dilemmas that imagination and foresight might have prevented.

To illustrate, consider the fictional challenge to one's moral imagination provided by a questionnaire in the journal *Chemical Engineering*.[10] In a case titled "The Falsified Data," Jay and his fellow catalyst experts find preliminary evidence that catalyst B is superior to catalyst A in a particular context. But Jay and the others (including the head of his group) are unanimously convinced that the evidence is unreliable and that, in fact, catalyst A is superior. The problem, they believe, is that the study was rushed and performed under less than ideal conditions. However, a decision about which catalyst to use must be made now. Jay's boss asks Jay to falsify the data by doing the math backward to show that A is superior to B. What should Jay do?

When we presented this question to a group of engineering students at our university, more than half indicated that they would falsify the data as instructed. We then presented the sequel, "The Falsified Data Strike Back." Jay has falsified the data. But much to his dismay, he later discovers that although catalyst A usually is superior to catalyst B, in the circumstances in question B is superior to A. Now what should Jay do? One of the students quickly replied, "I'd go back to the first case!" Of course, in a real-life situation, one cannot go back and undo the previous decision. Jay does have alternatives besides falsifying the data or refusing to do what he is told. For example, he might suggest to his boss that they acknowledge the initial evidence in favor of B but go ahead and recommend A anyway (on the basis of their previous experience).

These two cases suggest the importance of anticipating the need to make recommendations so that enough time is set aside for more careful studies than Jay and his associates had undertaken. This foresight is what might be called *preventive ethics*: anticipating needs in such a way that one will not be faced with an ethical dilemma later.

Recognizing Ethical Issues

Appraising your immediate responses, identifying unstated assumptions, and asking whether a visceral response alone can be the basis of a moral judgment are all part of this recognition process.

It is important not only to evaluate one's immediate reactions to situations but also to recognize when moral assessment of a situation is called for. We do not always recognize the moral dimensions of a situation. For example, the use of deception was until quite recently regarded by many social scientists as an acceptable element of experimental design.[11] Similarly, the use of placebos and various forms of paternalistic deception in medical practice have only recently been subjected to careful moral scrutiny.

Sometimes recognizing the ethical dimensions of a situation requires the assistance of someone who is less involved in it. For example, one of the authors witnessed the following conversation between the other author and a car repairman. Pritchard's car had a stalling problem, and he was picking it up after being told that the bill was ready.

PRITCHARD: My billing says that I need to order a part in order to adequately correct the problem. Can I drive the car in the meantime?

REPAIRMAN: That depends on how much you need to drive.

PRITCHARD: I don't need to drive so much that I'm willing to have the car stall on a main street like it did yesterday.

REPAIRMAN: Well, it's really up to you.

PRITCHARD: Would you drive the car if it were yours?

REPAIRMAN: That depends on how much I needed it to drive.

PRITCHARD: Have you done anything to correct the problem temporarily, or will the car drive just like it did when I brought it in this morning?

REPAIRMAN: Nothing we did today will make it behave any differently, if that's your question. You need to order the part to fix the problem.

Because Jaksa had taken Pritchard to pick up his car, Pritchard was able to get a ride home and leave his car until the part arrived. He was also treated to an unexpected lecture about ethics.

JAKSA: That was incredible! He was willing to let you drive your car out of there without even telling you it wasn't any better than before. Talk about ethically questionable communication!

PRITCHARD: I was so intent on finding out if the car was safe enough to drive that I didn't even think about the ethics of the situation.

JAKSA: He knew the car was the same. But he wasn't going to tell you unless you asked. Even worse, he didn't care what you did. That's really irresponsible. What if you had driven away and had an accident?

After a moment's reflection, Pritchard agreed. Although the repairman had not actually lied, his behavior was deceptive. Pritchard had been billed for services rendered. Admittedly, the bill indicated the need for further work. It might be suggested that the repairman behaved responsibly in making that notation on the bill. However, when one relies on the technical expertise of others, one must be given all relevant information. Even though the customer has a responsibility to ask questions pertaining to safety, the mechanic has a responsibility to communicate relevant safety information promptly and directly.

Developing Analytical Skills

This goal involves examining fundamental ethical concepts such as justice, utility, rights, duties, self-respect, respect for others, dignity, autonomy, informed consent, and paternalism to see to what extent these concepts can be applied consistently and coherently in similar cases. Learning what kinds of arguments and justifications best support your moral assertions is also important.

Consider this hypothetical example.[12] A traffic safety supervisor has to recommend safety improvements at either a busy urban intersection or a more remote rural intersection. The annual number of fatal accidents at each intersection is virtually identical, although the number of accidents resulting in property damage and minor injuries at the urban intersection is substantially greater. Which improvement should be recommended, given that only one improvement can be made at this time? Of course, more details about each intersection need to be known. But one of the issues that must be raised is how utility (the greatest good for the greatest number) should be ranked with fairness to individuals at risk. Utility would seem to favor the urban intersection, because more people benefit from the improvement. However, those traveling through the rural intersection are at much greater individual risk of having a fatal accident. Further, some consideration must be given to the value of saving lives compared with the value of preventing property damage and minor injuries.

Tolerating Disagreement

Even if ethical certainty is often impossible, ethical reasoning about choices can be made somewhat precise. Tolerating differences of choice and refraining from automatically labeling opposite choices as immoral are essential. At the same time, seeking exact points of difference can help solve disagreements by eliminating false distinctions and evasions.

This fourth objective is particularly important for students of communication. Meeting this objective requires certain communication skills as well as analytical abilities. Good listening is crucial, as is the willingness and ability to engage in reflective conversation with others, even when their views differ significantly from one's own. At the same time, an overly accommodating attitude is to be avoided. It is sometimes tempting to respond to those with whom one differs with remarks such as, "Everyone's entitled to an opinion," "It's really just a matter of opinion," or "Value judgments are subjective."

Such statements tend to bring discussion quickly to an end. Although these statements seem to express an attitude of tolerance, they also suggest that we do not have much to learn from one another. But appraisals of our moral beliefs are rich in conversational possibilities. Quite apart from the question of whether our beliefs are "true" or "correct," we can evaluate their internal consistency and coherence, their comprehensiveness, their clarity and articulateness, their supporting reasons, the extent to which they exhibit careful reflection, and so on.

Moral Relativism

Another common response to moral disagreement and ambiguity is that morality "is all relative." But relative *to what*? Once this question is asked, the claim that morality is "relative" becomes in need of clarification. We will briefly consider three forms that moral relativism might take.

Conventionalist Relativism

This view holds that what is right or wrong, good or bad, and so on is decisively determined by the settled habits, traditions, and conventions of one's particular culture or society.

The view of conventionalist relativism may seem to have the virtue of tolerance, because it acknowledges that different cultures are each, in their own way, right. However, if each culture is right, nothing can be wrong with a culture that has a moral principle of intolerance (and even violence) toward other cultures.

Conventionalist relativism also permits intolerance toward dissenting minorities within a culture. Thus, morality is essentially conservative, and the idea of moral progress within a particular society is a myth. Abolishing slavery and granting women the right to vote may be cited as marks of moral progress. However, in the conventionalist view, they are simply marks of moral change, and until the majority agreed with these changes, advocates of these moral reforms apparently were behaving immorally.

Of course, in some circumstances, we might not think of tolerance as a virtue. The Nazi extermination of millions of Jewish people in the 1930s is now nearly universally condemned. But in the conventionalist view, if the Nazis could be said to have constituted a culture or society, such condemnation has no valid ground—what the Nazis did was, *for them*, as right as anything could be.

It might be argued that the Nazis did not constitute a culture, but only a (powerful) *segment* of a culture. This only raises a deeper question: What is a culture or society? Within any modern society, strands of several cultures might be found, and societies themselves are interdependent in ways that make it difficult to identify the kind of unified moral beliefs and practices presupposed by conventionalist relativism. Furthermore, an individual might have loyalties to a variety of cultural or societal groups that, at times, are in moral conflict with one another. How is such an individual to decide what to do?

Finally, even if the problem of cultural or societal identity can be resolved, conventionalist relativism has another disturbing feature. Individual judgment is subordinated to the "group," which is accorded the (admittedly "relative") status of having *moral infallibility*, no matter how morally offensive some of its practices might seem to its critics.

Individualist Relativism

Those who wish to avoid the conventionalist relativist suppression of individual judgment might prefer this form of relativism. However, individualist relativism replaces the moral infallibility of the group with the moral infallibility of the individual. In this view, "thinking it's so makes it so" in moral matters. To the question "Who's to judge?" the individualist relativist has a ready answer: "I am, for me. And you are, for you." Individuals are morally infallible insofar as they conform to their genuine, individual moral beliefs, whatever their content.

If each of us is right in his or her way, we cannot have much to say to one another about moral matters. This view, like conventionalist relativism, may seem to have the virtue of tolerance. But if someone believes intolerance toward others is all right, it is morally acceptable (for that person). Individualist relativism does respect the autonomy of the individual insofar as it rejects deference to the moral authority of other individuals or groups. However, the view seems to turn the virtue of autonomy into the vice of *moral arrogance*, since one can do no wrong as long as one is "true to oneself."

Situationist Relativism

In this popularly supported view, morality is "relative to the situation." If that phrase simply meant that moral judgments need to take into account the special features of the matters that judgments are made about, it would be true enough. However, something more controversial is often meant— that each situation is unique, so that moral principles are useless and generalizations to other situations are inappropriate. Like conventionalist and individualist relativism, situationist relativism really leaves little room for discussion. Taken to the extreme, no general criteria for moral judgment are available.

Moral Relativism vs. Nonrelativism

One reason many people are attracted to some form of moral relativism is that they are troubled by what they think nonrelativism entails. However, nonrelativism is often misunderstood. We will address three common misunderstandings.

1. Nonrelativists are often suspected of intolerance toward those whose moral beliefs and values differ from theirs. No doubt some are intolerant in this way. But not all nonrelativists think that they have all (or even many of) the answers to moral questions. They can be open to being persuaded that they are mistaken. What they are committed to is the belief that some moral views are more acceptable than others—whether they, or anyone else, currently subscribe to the most acceptable views.

2. Nonrelativists are often accused of being *absolutists* who believe that exceptionless moral principles exist, such as "Never lie," "Never kill," or "Never be cruel." But nonrelativists don't necessarily believe in absolutes in this sense. They do believe that some general principles, criteria, or values are universally *relevant* in making determinations of right, wrong, and so on. For example, a nonrelativist could

insist that the fact that something is a lie counts against it, even if other factors might be more decisive in a particular situation.

3. Nonrelativists are sometimes thought to have no respect for moral traditions, conventions, or practices. However, there is no reason nonrelativists cannot admit the relevance, and even the great importance, of moral traditions, conventions, and practices to questions of right and wrong. They simply refuse to accept the conventionalist view that these matters are necessarily decisive. Furthermore, even if nonrelativists think that some traditions, conventions, or practices are in some respects morally objectionable, it does not follow that they think it would be appropriate to intervene. Nonrelativists need not be any more interventionist than anyone else. In fact, they may often find it very difficult to justify imposing their values on other cultures. Respect for the integrity and ways of life of other cultures is itself a principle for which nonrelativist support can be given. Relativists cannot provide similar assurances.

Narrow vs. Broad Vision

We will close this chapter with an illustration of the difference between narrow and broad vision.[13] Imagine that a revolution has taken place in a certain country. The revolutionaries have decided that they need to dramatically demonstrate that the old regime is definitely out. So they select three representatives of the old regime for public execution by guillotine: a priest, a doctor, and an engineer. But this is to be no ordinary guillotining. Those to be executed are to lie on their backs and look up at the blade as it comes crashing down on them. First the priest is prepared for execution. The cord is pulled, and down comes the blade. But it stops eight inches from his neck. The revolutionaries are dumbfounded. How could this be? they ask. Then it occurs to them that because the priest is a man of God, perhaps this is a message. So they decide to spare the priest. Next is the doctor. The cord is pulled, but once again the blade stops eight inches from the doctor's neck. The revolutionaries are stunned. But they conclude that because the doctor is dedicated to healing, another message is being given. So they spare the doctor. Finally it is the engineer's turn. Just as the cord is about to be pulled, the engineer shouts, "Wait a minute. I think I see what the problem is." That is what is meant by narrow vision.

The engineer represents all of us insofar as we fail to see the broader implications of our actions when concentrating only on what is immediately before us. Courses in ethics cannot eliminate this problem. But, if well designed, they can help.

Discussion Questions

1. What are your expectations from a course in communication ethics?

2. Do you think it is important for students of communication to study ethics? Explain.

3. Think of several situations you have been involved in that you think have important ethical dimensions related to communication.

4. What do you think are the most significant areas of ethical concern in communication? Explain. Can you give examples?

5. You are a dinner guest. You know your host has tried very hard to prepare a delicious meal. But you find the food very unappealing. The host, apparently anxious for comments, asks you, "How is the food?" What do you say?

6. You feel rotten but do not wish to discuss this with anyone at this time. An acquaintance comes up to you and asks, "How are you?" What do you say?

7. You are taking a test. The person next to you asks the answer to one of the questions. What should you do? Does it matter if the person is a friend?

8. Jill has forgotten to write her take-home essay. Instead of admitting this to her teacher, she says: "I wrote my essay, but I forgot to bring it to class today. May I bring it in tomorrow?" Discuss.

9. "People usually want to know the truth, even if it hurts, because they don't like to be duped or left in the dark. Of course, if they'll never find out they're being duped, then it's all right to deceive them." Discuss.

10. Is it morally objectionable to tell a potential buyer that $45,000 is the lowest price for which you will sell your house when you know you will settle for less?

11. Is it morally objectionable for a 56-year-old person who looks and feels many years younger to lie about his or her age to a prospective employer—because of a fear that the employer would prefer a younger person?

12. If the 56-year-old person does lie, is hired, performs well on the job for several years, but then is found to have lied, what should that person do? What should the employer do?

Law School Admissions I

You are applying to law school. You know that you will be admitted only if you get a strong letter of recommendation from Professor Johnson, because your Law School Admissions Test scores are only marginally acceptable to law schools. You honestly believe that you can do well—if only you are accepted. Still, you know that you have not been an outstanding student in Professor Johnson's classes. Even though you received A's and B's, so did many others. You notice that the recommendation form asks for a ranking of the candidate in comparison with other students the professor has had: top 5 percent; top 10 percent; top 25 percent; top 50 percent; bottom 50 percent. Your honest estimate of your ranking is that you are somewhere in the top 25 percent, but clearly below the top 10 percent.

But you are quite convinced that if you are not ranked in at least the top 10 percent, you very likely will not be accepted into law school. If you are ranked in the top 5 percent, you think that your chances will be quite good, for the following reason. For several years, law schools have received inflated letters of recommendation. The percentile ranking system was introduced to combat this inflationary trend, but it has continued. Law schools know that the number of students recommended as being in the top 5 or 10 percent is greatly exaggerated. So you fear that if you are ranked by Professor Johnson as only being in the top 25 percent, law schools will "translate" this to the top 50 percent at best. How truthful do you think Professor Johnson's ranking and letter should be? Discuss.

The Placebo I

You have not been feeling well for some time now. You are alternately tense and fatigued. Some nights you lie awake; the next day you find yourself drooping on the job—even snoozing during breaks. You frequently have headaches and an upset stomach. The first doctor who examined you did not find anything physically wrong. You now have an appointment with a new doctor. If your new doctor cannot find anything physically wrong with you, would she be justified in deceiving you by giving you a placebo if she honestly thinks that doing so will enable you to overcome your problems? If so, what should she say to you?

15

A CRISIS
OF CONFIDENCE?

A recent *New Yorker* cartoon depicts a boardroom meeting in which someone announces: "Of course, honesty is one of the better policies." We find it wryly amusing that honesty is acknowledged to be merely a practical option rather than a moral imperative. Presented as a matter of business policy, honesty loses its moral luster and has to fight it out on even terms with other practical policies. Our amused reaction suggests that we are not taken in by the nostrum "Honesty is the best policy."

Our amusement at the *New Yorker* cartoon reveals a certain cynicism about the level of honesty we expect from leaders in government, business, and the professions. If the national opinion polls of recent years are to be believed, we are in the grip of pervasive doubt about the trustworthiness of these leaders.

At the outset of her book *Lying: Moral Choice in Public and Private Life*, Sissela Bok notes the astonishment many felt at learning in 1960 that President Dwight D. Eisenhower had lied about the U-2 incident, in which Gary Powers and his spy plane had been forced down in the Soviet Union. "But," Bok continues, "only fifteen years later, battered by revelations about Vietnam and Watergate, 69 percent of the respondents to a national poll agreed that 'over the last ten years, this country's leaders have consistently lied to the people.'"[1]

The Vietnam war era was one of the most bitter and controversial periods in American history. The gap between what was said by government officials and what was believed by the public was immense, contributing significantly to the public's diminished confidence in its government leaders.

Bok mentions a memo written by a State Department official in September 1964 urging President Johnson to escalate the war.[2] However, because Johnson was portraying his political opponent Barry Goldwater as an "irresponsible war hawk," the memo urged that the escalation be kept secret from the public. Apparently following the advice of the memo, Johnson consistently described himself as the candidate of peace. The strategy succeeded: Johnson was re-elected and the war was soon escalated. The expression *credibility gap* was coined during the continued expansion of the war amid public demonstrations and rioting.

Watergate and Its Legacy

"Just destroy all the tapes."
—Unindicted coconspirator Richard M. Nixon, asked at a recent press luncheon about what he thought was the greatest lesson of Watergate.[3]

On June 17, 1972, burglars hired by the Committee for the Re-election of the President (Richard Nixon) broke into the national committee headquarters of the Democratic Party, located in the Watergate complex in Washington, D.C. What ensued in the following two years was a national nightmare. The Watergate burglary and the unraveling cover-up dominated the attention of an entire nation. Americans watched the Watergate hearings on national television for hundreds of hours, as prominent members of the Nixon administration were grilled by the Senate investigating committee. By the end of the ordeal, *Watergate* had become a household word. Careers were destroyed, families were broken, prison sentences were imposed, and the president's administration was in disarray.

The nation felt scorn, anger, disappointment, shock, and disbelief that so many crimes, and so much intentional deception, could have been committed by a presidential administration. Through it all, the president maintained his innocence, despite overwhelming testimony that caused the Senate investigating committee, the public, and other special investigating bodies to believe otherwise. Finally, under pressure from the House Judiciary Committee, which voted to recommend impeachment, and in the face of the revelations of the White House tapes, Richard Nixon resigned his office on August 9, 1974.

Public trust had been shattered. The deceit had been so widespread that the public wondered how long it might be before a semblance of trust in the highest levels of government could be restored.

Political Effects

In June 1982, ten years after the break-in, *Newsweek* tried to assess the residual effects of Watergate. What were Nixon's thoughts on Watergate a decade later? *Newsweek* printed his reply to Diane Sawyer's question during a *CBS Morning News* interview:

> I would say that, as far as the country is concerned, after the understandable reaction immediately with regard to politics generally, the castration of the CIA, the opposition to some of the attitudes toward the FBI, et cetera . . . the Watergate syndrome has probably run its course, and that is to the good.[4]

Although Sawyer was persistent in trying to get him to express further thoughts and feelings, Nixon refused: "As far as I'm concerned, I've said everything I can on the subject. Remember Lot's wife. Never look back."[5] Asked whether he would do anything differently if given the opportunity, he admitted, "Yes, we did make mistakes." One of the biggest ones, he indicated, was not destroying the tapes. Pressed by Sawyer in other areas, the former president repeatedly responded with statements such as, "No comment," "Well, I think we've covered enough," or "I've already pointed out that I'm not looking back."

Although Nixon was not inclined to reflect on Watergate and its effects on himself, on others in his administration, on government institutions, or on the general public, *Newsweek* did:

> Watergate was much more than a personal tragedy for a dishonored President: It was a rite of passage for the nation. And the "Watergate syndrome" . . . affected American institutions from the press to the presidency itself. Ten years after the June 17 break-in . . . the legacy is still strong. It has curbed the FBI and the CIA, awakened a dormant Congress, visited the "post-Watergate morality" upon big business, and drastically altered the ethical standards imposed on public officials at every level of government.[6]

The erosion of trust in government resulting from Watergate still poses a problem for members of Congress. Although some were not even in office during the affair, their credibility is hampered today. One Democratic state senator, Julian Bond of Georgia, remarked, "I think the general public thinks all of us are crooks, and I really reject that idea."[7] When *Newsweek* took a poll in 1973 that asked, "To what degree, if at all, has the Watergate situation reduced your confidence in the federal government as an institution?", 30 percent of the respondents said "a great deal" and 37 percent said "somewhat." Only 29 percent responded "not at all." In 1982,

21 percent said "a great deal," while 45 percent said "somewhat." Only 30 percent responded "not at all." These polls reflect very little change in attitude during that nine-year period. Apparently Watergate still significantly affects the degree of confidence people have in their government.

Frank Mankiewicz, former president of National Public Radio, political journalist, press secretary to Senator Robert Kennedy, and director of Senator George McGovern's 1972 presidential campaign, observed: "Nixon aides kept saying, 'We may have committed illegal, unconstitutional acts, and then lied and covered them up—but we were only doing what all leaders do.' And the American people somehow believed this." Mankiewicz contends that Americans have "a changed, less indignant attitude toward antisocial behavior in their leaders—from school boards to the president. Illegal, even criminal, acts seem to be regarded as the norm."

So indignation is replaced by a cynical indifference. Mankiewicz attributes voter apathy to this changed attitude. He concludes, "People don't think it matters who is elected; they think the alternatives are about the same. So they don't vote."[8] Those who do not vote, he adds, apparently do not care who wins. Such indifference reflects skepticism on the part of the public that their choice of candidates for public office is really a "significant choice."[9] Thus the meaningfulness of a generally valued right to exercise political choice appears to be endangered.

Public trust in, and respect for, elected officials is fundamental to the effective functioning of a democratic government and its institutions. Cynical indifference can be as inimical to democracy as outright opposition and hostility.

What has been the effect of Watergate on the presidency? Star Watergate witness John Dean said that there was "a surprising degree of continuity between one presidency and the next on what is acceptable conduct. Watergate snapped that continuity; it could have grown worse down the line."[10]

Newsweek observed: "When there was talk of sending U.S. troops to El Salvador, Reagan was reminded that the Oval Office is no longer the bully pulpit of Teddy Roosevelt's time—or even Lyndon Johnson's." Elizabeth Holtzman, a member of the House impeachment committee in 1974, added: "The President can no longer snap his fingers and expect the public to rally around him."[11] Thus the power of the presidency apparently has been kept in check at least partly as a result of Watergate, although observers may disagree about whether these limitations are desirable.

What are the effects of Watergate on those who participated in the break-in, authorized it, or helped in the cover-up? Several went to jail. All lost political power, and none have returned to public affairs. This roster includes many of the most powerful individuals in the Nixon administration, such as former Attorney General John Mitchell, chief of staff H. R. Halde-man, adviser John Ehrlichman, John Dean, and public relations specialist Jeb Stuart Magruder (whose Watergate experience is detailed in Chapter 9). Most have talked about the personal harms they and their families suffered.

The Press

The effects of Watergate on the press have been considerable. The relationship between the press and public officials in a democracy is generally characterized by tension. The job of the press has been seen as representing the public's interest in vital information and "keeping politicians honest." But prior to Watergate, government officials had been successful in controlling the press in wartime, citing security concerns. The abuse of power during Watergate, the unwillingness of the White House to provide the press and the nation with information, and the rampant deceit all prompted the press to more aggressively assert its responsibility to the public.

Robert Woodward and Carl Bernstein broke the Watergate story for the *Washington Post*, using an aggressive, combative, and even dangerous style of reporting. This style, now well known as investigative reporting, is being used by more and more reporters. Public officials feel they are under continual scrutiny. Some complain that the press has gone too far, even to the extent of invading privacy. John Connally, former U.S. Treasury Secretary and former governor of Texas, has noted: "Everyone is now afraid. People are fearful about the phone call they make. They worry whether a visitor is wearing a hidden mike."[12]

But journalists contend that this adversarial relationship between the press and public officials is better than "the bad old days" when cozy relationships between officials and reporters led to blindly one-sided, naive reports. Under those conditions, they maintain, the public was not adequately informed. Nicholas Horrock of the *New York Times* has characterized this change in relationship as fundamental and constructive: "A lot of young reporters today are more likely to ask the right questions of the right people than before Watergate."[13]

But public doubt extends to the press as well as government. In a May 1981 Gallup poll, 52 percent of the respondents said they believe only some of the news they read and hear. Given the complexity of many newsworthy items, this is perhaps not surprising. However, more significant is the assertion by 33 percent of the respondents that they believe reporters often make things up.

The legacy of Watergate is a changed nation, one that is more skeptical of itself and its institutions and less naive about political practices. However, the effects may not all be negative. *Newsweek* concluded its article on a somewhat optimistic note: "The fact that Americans are still examining themselves and their institutions as a result of the national nightmare that began a decade ago is perhaps as important as any of Watergate's lasting effects."[14]

The Iran-Contra Affair

President Ronald Reagan's first term in office was marked by a significant increase in public confidence in government leaders. However, just as it seemed that public cynicism was on the wane, the *New York Times* reported that a Lebanese weekly magazine, *Al Shiraa*, had published a story claiming that the United States had secretly sold arms to Iran.[15] The State Department immediately denied the allegation. Reagan admitted that arms had been sent to Iran, but he played down the amount, saying that the entire arms shipment "could be put in one cargo plane, and there would be plenty of room left over."[16] This response was greeted with widespread skepticism.

Critics quickly began making comparisons with the Nixon years, dubbing the current controversy "Irangate," thus providing fresh evidence that Watergate had not been forgotten, even in late 1986. Suddenly the Reagan administration was in the midst of a scandal that cast serious doubt on its credibility. Congress and members of the American public were enraged. So were U.S. allies throughout the world. The U.S. government had insisted that they would not deal for hostages, but it was quickly determined that the administration had sold arms to Iran in the hope that the Iranians could arrange the release of U.S. hostages held in the Middle East.

A congressional committee immediately began looking into the affair. Under pressure, Reagan established his own investigating committee, the Tower Commission. The press published investigative reports. Bit by bit, the details began to emerge. Indeed, the United States had arranged for shipments of arms valued at $100 million to the Iranians, through the cooperation of Israel, at least seven times between August 30, 1985, and October 29, 1986.

The shock of these revelations had not yet settled when another startling discovery was made. The payments from the arms-to-Iran deal had been deposited in a Swiss bank account and then redirected to aid the

Contras, rebel forces fighting the socialist government in Nicaragua, circumventing official U.S. government policies and procedures.

Initial disclosures indicated that the entire affair was under the direction of a low-level officer in the National Security Council, Lt. Col. Oliver North, whose office was in the White House basement. North was under the immediate command of Vice Adm. John Poindexter, the NSC adviser. Former NSC adviser Robert (Bud) McFarlane had also figured prominently in the operation. Both North and Poindexter were fired. Over the next several months, investigators would try to untangle the mess and determine who else was involved.[17]

The Tower Commission report dealt a further blow to the Reagan administration. It concluded that the president "clearly didn't understand what was going on; he let his emotions rule him, never ordered a critical review and allowed his aides to manipulate him and make their own foreign policy as they lied, diverted arms profits and tried to cover up the scandal."[18]

The president's own testimony before the Tower Commission was filled with inconsistencies, further damaging his credibility. He first told the commission that he had approved of the August 1985 shipment of arms. Then, after a White House staff briefing, he changed his mind, saying that he had not given approval. He later sent a letter to the commission, saying that he had let others influence his recollection. He declared, "The simple truth is, I don't remember, period."[19]

As far as the public was concerned, the polls told the story. Only 10 percent believed that he was telling the truth about the diversion of funds to the Contras. Only 23 percent believed that he was doing all he could to uncover the facts of the situation.[20]

The Joint Senate-House Investigating Committee held eleven weeks of public televised hearings during the summer of 1987. Numerous figures associated with the Reagan administration were questioned, including MacFarlane, North, Poindexter, Major General Richard Secord, Secretary of State George Schultz, Secretary of Defense Caspar Weinberger, former White House Chief of Staff Donald Regan, and Attorney General Edwin Meese. What the public heard was a shocking record of lies and deceit. There were "lapses of memory" of key witnesses and stories of the shredding, burning, and falsifying of important government documents. Poindexter testified that he withheld information from the president in order to "protect him" from being held responsible for sending money to the Contras. Secretary of State Schultz provided an astounding account of intrigue, deception, and "guerilla warfare" inside the Reagan administration. He called it "a battle royal."[21]

After the hearings concluded in early August of 1987, an ABC News poll showed that 52 percent of the American public still believed that the president was not telling the truth about what he had known.[22] Although no "smoking gun" was found to implicate the president, *Newsweek* concluded that "there is nevertheless no doubt that Reagan is a diminished president. His own polls continue to reflect lingering public skepticism about his credibility."[23]

As the president had promised, he spoke to the nation about the Iran-Contra affair in a televised address on August 12, 1987, when he accepted responsibility for the arms-to-Iran deal. He admitted that his concern for the hostages may have resulted in some bad judgment. He criticized Poindexter for not discussing with him the diversion of funds to the Contras. "The buck stops with me," said the president. "I had the right, the obligation to make my own decision."

The speech was brief, leaving many questions unanswered. An NBC poll, conducted the following morning, indicated that 55 percent of the public still did not believe that the president told the whole story.[24] Reporters on NBC's *Today Show* asked Chief of Staff Howard Baker if he thought the speech would accomplish the president's objective of putting the Iran-Contra affair behind him. Baker not only expressed doubts about this but also added that "in years to come, this will be discussed by him and others."[25]

No doubt Baker is correct: As of this writing, the Joint Congressional Investigation Committee's Report has not been made public, and special prosecutor Lawrence Walsh's investigation has not been completed. Thus, like the U-2 incident, Vietnam, and Watergate, the Iran-Contra affair will go down as another major chapter in governmental deception. The cumulative effect of these deceptions contributes to a crisis of confidence in public officials and makes the restoration of trust a serious challenge to American society.

Confidence in the Professions

The loss of confidence and trust in leaders is not confined to government. A Harris survey (see Table 2.1) compares the percentage of people with "a great deal of confidence" in the professions in 1966 and 1976.[26] Polls taken in subsequent years do not show a significant change from the 1976 percentages.

The July 1983 *Gallup Report* (#214) shows similar results. It closes by saying, "The current results show little change from those recorded in three previous surveys conducted since 1976." These results suggest that for some time now, the public has regarded the moral and ethical behavior of its leaders in government, business, and the professions as considerably

Table 2.1

	1966	1976
Medicine	73	42
Military	62	23
Education	61	31
Major companies	55	16
Organized religion	41	24
Press	29	20
Law firms	24	12
Organized labor	22	10
Ad agencies	21	7

less than exemplary. Because the viability of modern societies increasingly depends on these leaders and the institutions they represent, there are many who believe we are in the midst of a "crisis of confidence."

But some evidence indicates that leaders in government, business, and the professions do not fully appreciate the public's concern with honesty. The Connecticut Mutual Life Insurance Company commissioned a survey that asked the public to name the qualities they want most in "a leader for the nation." Connecticut Mutual's summary of the survey makes a disturbing observation:

> Far and away, the most frequently mentioned quality is honesty, followed (and not closely) by intelligence. Leaders, the report notes, underestimate the importance of this moral dimension; when asked what they feel the public looks for in a leader, leaders do not cite honesty among their top three choices.[27]

If dishonesty is a serious problem in our society, what kind of response is called for? Ivan Hill, founder of the Ethics Resource Center (American Viewpoint, Inc.), has recently suggested that 80–85 percent of the people must be honest 80–85 percent of the time in order to have an efficient, manageable, and open society.[28] Is this percentage likely to be sufficient? Imagine your best friend lying to you 15–20 percent of the time. How much confidence would you have in the word of your friend? Or imagine you were going to buy a car. How much confidence would you have in the advice of a salesperson you know lies 15–20 percent of the time? Quite apart from the 15–20 percent of the people Hill could accept as consistently dishonest, those who are honest only 80–85 percent of the time do not inspire much trust.

Ironically, some Ethics Resource Center interviews with corporate leaders strongly suggest that Hill has vastly underestimated the degree of honesty society requires. Interviewers asked 181 executives whether they believed their companies would benefit if their codes of ethics specifically stated that all information released to the public and all product or service advertising must be honest and forthright. Only 60 percent said yes; 35 percent said no.

These results do not necessarily mean that 35 percent are prepared to be dishonest about such matters. Some might believe that companies should be honest even if they do not directly benefit from it. Or some might believe that codes of ethics do not themselves influence behavior. Of course, some who believe that a statement of honesty in their code of ethics would benefit their company might view it simply as good public relations. They could, nevertheless, privately advocate violating the code whenever the company could get away with it. In any case, if even as many as 20 percent are prepared to permit dishonesty, or if the public *believes* that this many would permit dishonesty, what happens to the level of confidence and trust the public has in business and industry?

Once doubt sets in, credibility is difficult to regain. For example, in response to the first Tylenol scare, Johnson & Johnson immediately withdrew its inadequately packaged products from the market. Because several people had already died as a result of someone putting cyanide in the product while it was on store shelves, quick and decisive action on the part of the manufacturer was appreciated. The recall of the product and its prompt repackaging were very costly. Johnson & Johnson spokespersons explained that the company's action was a matter of social responsibility that overrode any concern for profit. But how likely is it that the public and the business world believed this explanation?

Skeptics speculated that from a cost-benefit standpoint, Johnson & Johnson had no choice but to immediately withdraw its product. In the long run, it would avoid possibly ruinous lawsuits and it would regain the confidence of the public in its product. All that we need credit Johnson & Johnson with, it might be argued, is an astute perception of the constraints of law and the market—and an opportunistic public relations tactic (the posture of social responsibility).

But what if Johnson & Johnson *does* take social responsibility seriously as a moral obligation to its customers? In the face of widespread skepticism, it can do little to convince the public that its honesty and ethical standards should be ranked "high" or "very high." Even if Johnson & Johnson does subscribe to the view that "Honesty is the best policy," the doubting public may smile cynically and translate this as, "Of course, honesty is one of the better policies."

Perceptions of Honesty

Are we in the midst of a crisis of confidence? More than half of those polled recently by *U.S. News & World Report* think that people are less honest today than they were just ten years ago, with seven out of ten saying that they are dissatisfied with current standards of honesty.[29] John Gardner, founder of Common Cause, thinks there is good reason for this public response: "Duplicity and deception, in public and private life, are very substantially greater than they have been in the past." Robert Nisbet, Columbia University's Albert Schweitzer Professor Emeritus, agrees: "The whole fabric of society has loosened a great deal, and there is consequently more lying."[30]

Of course, polls do not settle the question of whether people actually are less honest now than in the past. But even if these estimates are somewhat exaggerated, they do indicate a serious problem of public confidence. Gary Edwards, director of the Ethics Resource Center, warns:

> The stakes are high. A free and open society needs a high degree of ethical conduct, because people must have trust in their institutions and in the leaders of those institutions. . . . In business, where that doesn't happen, you lose economic freedom and get more regulation. In government, when trust and confidence break down, you get apathy, cynicism and, ultimately, anarchy.[31]

Why the public perceives deception to be increasing may be partly attributable to technology. *U.S. News* comments that while a politician used to be able to tell a "whopper" in the relative obscurity of a local whistle-stop, "today it may be bounced by satellite into millions of living rooms on the evening news."[32]

An additional factor is that the media are often a means of deception. Philosopher Christina Hoff Sommers comments that we are "constantly bombarded by information that's really disinformation." Television executive Jerry Femina concurs, adding: "We're conceived, born, and deceived. By the time someone reaches age 10, he's pretty cynical."[33]

But despite its cynicism, the public still holds honesty and integrity as a high priority. Seventy-two percent polled in the *U.S. News* survey said they believe that a president should never lie to the American public, and 59 percent said a president should never lie to a foreign government. In private life, honesty ranked the highest of all attributes or qualities in a friend. The next-highest-ranked attribute (a sense of humor) received considerably less support (49 percent).[34]

It may seem that we have painted a rather bleak picture of communication in public life. However, our intention has been to make clear why we believe the ethical issues addressed in subsequent chapters should be taken seriously. It is to those issues that we now turn.

Cheating: A New U.S. Fad?

Discuss the following case based on an article by Lidia Wasowicz, United Press International.[35]

ANAHEIM, CALIF.—Americans have turned deceit into a national "pastime," cheating on everything from diets to marriage partners and costing the government $100 billion a year in lost tax revenues, a leading psychologist says.

Dr. Hattye Liston, associate professor of psychology at North Carolina Agricultural and Technical State University, painted a "blatant, grotesque picture of cheating" at the 91st annual American Psychological Association convention Sunday.

"It's an American pastime, supported by inflation, cushioned on a recession which floats in all directions," she said.

"Cheating in America is epidemic and big business. It is a moral dilemma."

She cited statistics supporting her contentions:

- Tax cheating exceeds an estimated $100 billion a year.
- Pilferage costs department stores more than $4 billion annually.
- An estimated $1 million is paid each year to welfare double-dippers.

- Telephone misuse such as billing to other people's numbers amounts to some $1 million a year.
- About 60 percent of employees improperly use company and institutional postage meters.
- About 30 percent to 50 percent of scholars sabotage exams, laboratory experiments and term reports or reprogram computer tapes for bills and passing grades.
- Nearly half of those trying to lose weight cheat during their diets.
- Thousands of used cars are sold each year with the odometers rolled back.
- Students have defaulted on 14 percent of federal educational loans.
- Extramarital lovers: "No definite figures, but definitely epidemic proportions."

Liston suggested more frequent audits, better record keeping, stricter regulations and monitoring and FBI probes in cases of serious fraud.

Most important, she said, is the need for "positive moral growth" in society and public support for ethical growth.[35]

Recycling Letters

In the spring of 1982, a joint investigation by the Associated Press and the *Pontiac* (Illinois) *Daily Leader* revealed that Ann Landers had been recycling 15-year-old letters in her advice column. The investigators claimed that between April 1981 and April 1982, she ran 33 letters that had appeared in her daily column in late 1966 and early 1967. The recycled letters contained only slight changes in wording, names, and ages. She did not inform either her readers or the editors of the more than 1,000 newspapers carrying her column that she was reusing old letters.

Ann Landers had often said publicly that the letters in her column were authentic, and she often criticized Yale University students for trying to get inauthentic letters into her column. When confronted with the evidence, Landers readily admitted that she had recycled the letters. She said she would immediately stop the practice, adding that "my credibility is all I have."

In an interview with an AP reporter and assistant publisher James Pearre of the *Daily Leader*, Landers explained, "It started about a year and a half ago, while I was going through my scrapbooks to find some letters for short (telephone) spots I was doing for

Illinois Bell. When I saw a letter that was especially interesting, or made a point in a forceful way, I considered using it again."

She added that she had only infrequently used past letters and that she did not think the practice "extraordinary or unusual." She continued:

> I think people read my column for advice, guidance, amusement. . . . I don't think the reader cares. The important thing is to get the information out.
>
> I feel if I get the advice out in a way that is useful or powerful, then I think the technique doesn't matter.

Steve Jehorek, president and chief executive officer of Field Newspaper Syndicate, which distributes the Ann Landers column, said that editors of the syndicate had not been aware of the recycling. Had they been, he added, they would have advised her against using old letters without labeling them as such. However, reassured Jehorek, "The items are legitimate questions from readers of the Ann Landers column. They are not contrived or inaccurate and the advice in them stands. They are simply repeats."[36]

Discussion Questions

1. To what extent, if any, do you think Ann Landers underestimated the public's concern about whether the letters she publishes are current?

2. Do you think that her failure to put the dates on the recycled letters has damaged her credibility?

"Disinformation"

In August 1986 some Reagan administration officials told journalists that Libyan leader Col. Muammar el-Qaddafi was renewing his support for terrorism and that this action could lead to another American attack on Libya. Reports appeared in the *Wall Street Journal* and the *Washington Post*. However, other officials later conceded that there was no hard evidence that Qaddafi was renewing his support for terrorism, and they said that the United States had no plans for military action. On October 2, 1986, the *Washington Post* quoted a White House memorandum, purportedly written by national security adviser, Vice Adm. John Poindexter, that outlined a strategy that "combines real and illusionary events—through a disinformation program—with the basic goal of making Qaddafi think that there is a high degree of internal opposition to him within Libya, that his key trusted aides are disloyal, that the U.S. is about to move against him militarily." Part of the alleged plan was to plant false information in the press.

The White House denied that it had employed a "disinformation" program. However, Secretary of State George Shultz defended, in principle, the use of such a strategy. He quoted Winston Churchill: "In time of war, the truth is so precious, it must be attended by a bodyguard of lies."

A journalist referred to the allegation that the administration had employed a disinformation strategy as "a very serious charge." Shultz replied:

> Why is that a charge? If I were a private citizen reading about it, and I read that my government was trying to confuse somebody who was conducting terrorist acts and murdering Americans, I would say, "Gee, I hope it is true." I don't see why you think this is a charge.[37]

Discussion Questions

1. Under what kinds of conditions, if any, do you think a governmental disinformation strategy can be morally justified? On what principle(s) are you relying?
2. Discuss Winston Churchill's statement.
3. Evaluate George Shultz's defense of using a disinformation strategy.
4. Shultz neither affirmed nor denied that the administration had actually used a disinformation strategy. If, in fact, the administration did *not* use such a strategy, should he have said so?

A Resignation

On October 8, 1986, State Department spokesman Bernard Kalb resigned to protest "the reported disinformation program" used by the

Reagan administration against Qaddafi. Kalb would not confirm that the administration had actually used a disinformation program. He said that he had not knowingly participated in such a program. He asserted: "In taking this action, I want to emphasize that I am not dissenting from Secretary Shultz, a man of integrity, a man of credibility. Rather I am dissenting from the reported disinformation program." Reacting to Kalb's resignation, President Reagan commented, "No one on our side has been lying to anyone."

How did Kalb explain his resignation, if he was not directly confirming the existence of a disinformation program? Some of his public statements:

> Faith in the word of America is the pulsebeat of our democracy. Anything that hurts America's credibility hurts America. . . .
>
> My resignation does not endow me with sudden freedom to act on what may be or not be secret and what can be classified or what cannot be classified. . . .
>
> You face a choice—as an American, as a spokesman, as a journalist—whether to allow oneself to be absorbed in the ranks of silence, whether to vanish into unopposed acquiescence, or to enter a modest dissent. . . .
>
> I have been agonizing about this thing. I knew nothing about it. I was concerned. I was concerned with the impact of any such program on the credibility of the United States and the word of America and what the word of America means.
>
> And I was concerned about my own integrity. My own integrity means something to me personally, but in the grand scheme of things I'm a simple asterisk. What I know is I didn't want my own integrity to get scooped up in this controversy.[38]

Discussion Questions

1. Discuss the significance of Kalb's resignation.
2. Why do you think resigning was a matter of personal integrity for Kalb?

ETHICAL VALUES IN COMMUNICATION

If we say that we expect people to be honest with us, we could mean either of two things. We could mean that we believe that people really will, as a matter of fact, be honest with us. As we have seen in the last chapter, in this sense, the public has rather low expectations from those in government, business, and the professions. Or we could mean that, in an ethical sense, we think that others *should* be honest with us. Ethical expectations are what we believe people *ought* to do, even if this is not what they actually do. Thus one can say, without being contradictory, "I expect salespersons to treat me honestly, but I really don't trust them."

So, however honest we believe people actually to be, the ethical expectation of honesty remains high. In this chapter, we will shift our focus to this second sense of expectation. We will consider some fundamental ethical expectations that we have in communicating with one another. Although honesty is prominent among those expectations, other values will be considered as well.

Modes of Persuasion

In many communication situations, the intent of the speaker is primarily to inform. The speaker may be more or less successful in presenting the information clearly, accurately, or efficiently. The speaker is not necessarily trying to bring about immediate, or even long-run, changes in the actions or behavior of the listener.

But how do we respond when a salesperson tries to sell us a VCR we can't afford, or when our supervisor tries to get us to learn a new data processing system during our lunch hour or after work—for no additional pay? Here the intention is to *persuade*, not inform. The speaker wants us to do something he or she prefers. When this happens, we may become defensive.

We may do this because we suspect that the persuader is trying to manipulate us in ways we believe to be detrimental to our own preferences, interests, or well-being. This defensiveness is rather widespread—ranging from resistance to advertising and mass media "blitzes" to resistance to political and religious attempts to persuade or indoctrinate us. We may even resist friends' attempts to persuade us. Nevertheless, it cannot be seriously maintained that all persuasion is bad or undesirable. It is not even wholly avoidable. We are not totally self-sufficient; we must rely on one another to some extent for advice and services in meeting our basic needs and interests.

Given the fact that persuasion, for good or ill, is an inescapable part of our lives, what ethical expectations about the use of persuasion might be reasonable? Our defensiveness suggests that we believe persuasion threatens some basic values. We ordinarily value:

- Truthful, relevant information that makes rational, significant choice possible.
- A range of alternatives to choose from.
- Sufficient time to reflect, consult with others, and respond.
- A presentation of the best reasons, rather than just those the persuader thinks will "work" with us.
- Being seen, and respected, as capable of making rational choices, rather than either as manipulatable "tools" of the persuader for personal gain or as objects of paternalistic concern.

When we discover that those attempting to persuade us are not taking these values into account, we feel our ethical expectations have been disappointed.

Kenneth Andersen characterizes persuasion as "communication in which the communicator seeks through the use of symbolic agencies, particularly language, to effect a desired voluntary change in the attitudes and/ or actions of the receiver(s)."[1] This characterization emphasizes the importance of *voluntary* change in the person being persuaded. It distinguishes persuasion from indoctrination or coercion, which do not allow significant choice. But it also suggests that ethically acceptable modes of persuasion do not rely on deceptive manipulative tactics. Andersen goes on to say:

Persuasion is a communication activity that unites people—yet it also permits maximum individual choice. It recognizes that people have a right and responsibility for their choices.[2]

Andersen views persuaders and their audiences as *coparticipants* in communication. Listeners should have considerable power to accept, select, or reject any or all of what is recommended by a persuader:

Functioning at its best, it [persuasion] both affirms and contributes to the mutual respect and self-respect of those jointly participating in the persuasion process.[3]

This approach to persuasion is a far cry from the defensive posture described at the outset of this section. While simply dropping one's defenses would be naive in our current environment, striving to move in the direction of Andersen's ideal seems to us to be morally desirable. If the ethical values he describes were a consistent part of the persuasion process, persuasion could be endorsed as an important, desirable, and viable part of social and political life.

We support those forms of persuasion that show respect for individuals as capable of making significant choices. Not all choices can, or even should, be based on evidence or proof. Rational argument is not the only morally acceptable form of persuasion. However, even when evidence or proof is not available, those capable of rational choice are respected only if manipulative and deceptive persuasive tactics are avoided. For example, one might be persuaded to buy a car not because it can be proved to be the "best" car on the market, but because it is aesthetically pleasing. While not necessarily interested in having the "best" car on the market, the buyer would, nevertheless, be upset to learn that the car gets only 14 miles per gallon when it was advertised as getting 30 miles per gallon.

What are some of the characteristics of ethically preferred persuasion? We will identify five.

1. The use of persuasion should reinforce, or at least be consistent with, democratic processes in a free society. Dissent, discussion, argument, debate, and persuasion in general are fundamental democratic values. However, when communication fails to permit listeners to make rational choices, freedom itself is endangered. Freedom of speech is an important right, but it also carries with it important responsibilities.

2. We value persuaders who demonstrate good character and good will. We respond favorably to persuaders who integrate personal integrity with the integrity of ideas. We appreciate persuaders who first conduct careful and conscientious research before attempting "to make

truth effective."[4] We want persuaders to be honest, disclosing important and relevant information for the case at hand. The great Roman teacher Quintilian summarized these qualities in saying, "The perfect orator is a good man speaking well."[5]

3. Those who attempt to persuade others should consider the varying perspectives of listeners and others who may be affected by the communication. We respect persuaders who demonstrate that they can view a situation through the eyes of listeners as well as their own. Deceivers tend to see things from their own, often quite restricted, perspectives.

4. Both the means and ends of persuasive communication should be ethically acceptable. The means of communication include the methodological choices of the persuader—the selection of material, the testing and arrangement of ideas, the intentions of the communicator, and the use of language and delivery. The ends include the effects that result from the persuader's presentation. Are they beneficial or harmful? Does the persuasion bring about long-range, positive effects, or does a "quick fix" result in harm over the long term?

5. Responsibility for communication does not rest solely on the speakers. Listeners and even those not directly involved in particular communication situations also have responsibilities. Kenneth Andersen emphasizes the voluntariness of listener responses in persuasive communication, suggesting that listeners should not view themselves as passive and uncritical receivers. Nonparticipants, who have opportunities to evaluate persuasive communication even though it is not addressed directly to them, also have responsibilities.[6] Voting, writing letters of opposition, or joining with others in organized protest are only some of the ways nonparticipants can exercise responsibility in opposing questionable modes of persuasion.

Mary John Smith supports Andersen's view of the listener as an active rather than a merely passive receiver of messages sent by persuaders. She contrasts transactional and "hypodermic" models of persuasion:

The transactional model of communication regards the communicative act as one in which two or more persons engage in mutual and simultaneous interaction and influence. Similarly, a transactional model of persuasion assumes that persuasive effects are the joint product of symbolic interaction between two or more persons and that each party shares a perception of choice and a sense of control over the persuasive encounter. . . . In contrast, the hypodermic model, like the hypodermic needle theory of persuasion, considers persuasion a unidirectional process whereby a source influences a relatively passive recipient. The receiver is regarded as a reactive victim of persuasive strategies, not as a full partner in the process of social influence.[7]

No simple answer can be given to the question of how much (and what kind of) responsibility speakers, listeners, and nonparticipants should accept in various circumstances. Richard Johannesen offers this answer: "[An] image of persuadees as active participants may suggest several responsibilities, perhaps captured by two phrases: Reasoned skepticism and appropriate feedback."[8]

The extent to which "reasoned skepticism" is a desirable attitude to have toward persuaders would seem to depend on the relationship between persuader and persuadee. Such an attitude seems reasonable enough in the areas of public speaking, advertising, business transactions, and perhaps in professional–client relationships. Receivers can inform themselves, ask questions, seek alternative sources of information, and generally be on guard in trying to determine the reliability of others' communications.

But this kind of defensiveness can interfere with more intimate relationships, in which mutual trust is essential. Even here, however, "appropriate feedback" signaling that the receiver is not naive or blindly acceptant has its place. The basic point in all instances is that receivers should regard themselves as being responsible for encouraging nondeceptive, nonmanipulative communication.

Truthfulness as a Norm

Although the level of public confidence in the ethical standards and honesty of leaders in government, business, and the professions is disturbingly low, we can imagine societies in which matters could be much worse. But how pervasive can untruthfulness be in a viable society? Can we imagine a society in which lying rather than truthfulness is the social and moral norm, in which lying would be judged morally acceptable, not just occasionally, but nearly without exception?

Such a society is almost impossible to conceive. Yet the Ik society, described in Colin Turnbull's *The Mountain People*, seems to come very close.[9] But the Ik society is presented as being on the verge of self-destruction. Untruthfulness among the Ik is just one of the many manifestations of the instability of the society, which is depicted as desperately trying to survive in the face of insurmountable physical obstacles, including the lack of arable land. Distrust and hostility among the Ik are so prevalent that it seems only a matter of time before the Ik society will cease to function.

But even among the Ik, lying cannot be said to constitute a nearly exceptionless norm. If a lie is to be successful, the liar must exploit the listener's normal expectation that the speaker is not only using words with their conventionally accepted meanings, but also that he or she is speaking truthfully. So it seems that not only can lying not be a nearly exceptionless norm, precisely the opposite must be the case if successful lying is to take place. That is, a general presumption against lying must be shared by a society in order for lying to be successful.

Peter Winch makes an even stronger claim: that the very possibility of a society depends on the general acceptance of truthfulness as a moral norm. Individual members of a society can, of course, deliberate at any particular moment about whether or not to speak truthfully. But as speakers of the language, they will already have learned what telling the truth is. Learning to speak, Winch claims, "involves at the same time learning that speaking truthfully is the norm and speaking untruthfully a deviation."[10]

Winch considers two suppositions that might be offered against the idea that speaking truthfully must be the norm in any society. First, suppose that what we now think of as false statements were always spoken in place of what we now think of as true statements, and vice versa. All that would result, Winch says, is that we would come to take statements in the opposite way to how we now take them. So the idea of lying being the norm is self-defeating. What if we suppose, however, that the incidence of true and false statements is statistically random, rather than systematically true or false? Then, says Winch, no distinction could be made between truth and falsity at all and, therefore, no communication could take place: "For to communicate it must be possible for people's utterances to be taken in certain specific ways by other people."[11]

So, although the particular language shared within any given society will be governed by certain linguistic conventions, adherence to the norm of truthfulness is not itself a matter of convention. This can be contrasted with norms that clearly are conventional, such as which side of the road to drive on—or even the existence of "rules of the road." These rules are conventional in the sense that they are explicitly agreed to, and we could imagine societies agreeing to significantly different rules—or perhaps, in some instances, not even having rules concerning such matters at all. But, without the norm of truthfulness, Winch contends, a shared language would not be possible.

But why must this norm of truthfulness be regarded as a *moral* norm? One might claim, Winch suggests, that the norm of truthfulness requires only that language be used correctly. Correct usage involves staying within the rough boundaries of conventionally accepted grammatical structures and the conventional meanings of words and sentences. Incorrect usage violates norms of language, but it is not necessarily morally objectionable. Although Winch agrees that the existence of a shared language does require correct usage, he points out that lying does not involve the incorrect use of language. In fact, in order to make any statement at all (truthful or otherwise), one must use language more or less correctly. The victim of a lie certainly understands what the liar has *said*. The success of the lie depends on this:[12]

> But there is something about the situation that he has failed to understand; and this we might express by saying he has failed to understand the *speaker*, in the sense that he has failed to understand what the speaker has *done*, or where the speaker stands. And this understanding of the role played by the speaker of an utterance is an essential part of language. Communication is not *just* understanding and using words.

How are we to understand the role played by the speaker? Those who share a language not only use language more or less correctly, they also indicate to others through their words that they are *committed* to a belief in what they say—even if they are speaking untruthfully. Winch continues: "One is committed by one's words and deeds and, given these, one cannot in addition *will* that one shall or shall not be committed in certain ways."[13] The moral objection to the liar is that he or she is letting down those with whom a commitment *has* been made.

Winch distinguishes between *what words mean* and *what people mean by words*. People can say and mean something only "in a society where people are so related that for one person to say something is for him to commit himself with others; and an important part of such a relation is that there should be a common respect for truthfulness."[14]

This common respect for truthfulness is not present in all exchanges, of course. For example, Senator Joe McCarthy, who conducted Communist "witch hunts" in the 1950s, was noted for his ability to manipulate the reactions of others, without himself being subject to similar reactions. Winch cites Richard Rovere's commentary on McCarthy:

> Basically, of course, he was a great sophisticate in human relationships, as every demagogue must be. He knew a great deal about people's fears and anxieties, and he was a superb juggler of them. But he was himself numb to the sensations he produced in others. He could not comprehend true outrage, true indignation, true anything.[15]

However, McCarthy's success was possible only because others do have tendencies to react with true outrage and indignation. His tactics exploited the fact that most people did not share his essentially manipulative view of communication. Winch comments:

> McCarthy's use of the "paraphernalia of rationality"—stuffed briefcase, footnotes, etc.—in order to impress people presupposed the existence of the real thing: something that could not be accounted for in terms of its usefulness in getting people to do and believe certain desired things, but which implies that certain values are respected for their own sakes.[16]

Winch's central moral claim is that no human society can exist in which truthfulness is not in general regarded as a virtue. While some lies might be justifiable, Winch holds that "a lie always needs special justification if it is not to be condemned."[17] Part of what is at stake is the viability of society. Another part is the integrity of the speaker. As Winch puts it:

> [*I*]*ntegrity* . . . is to human institutions generally what truthfulness is to the institution of language. . . . [T]he concept of integrity is inseparable from that of commitment. To lack integrity is to act with the appearance of fulfilling a certain role but without the intention of shouldering the responsibilities to which that role commits one. If that, *per absurdum*, were to become the rule, the whole concept of a social role would thereby collapse.[18]

Winch is not saying that an individual who lies will actually cause social breakdown. Only rarely could an individual lie have such an impact. Rather, his point is that each of us is part of a social network that depends on widespread observance of, and respect for, the norm of truthfulness. Those who make exceptions of themselves are dependent on others' commitment to this norm, and the more deviations there are, the more precarious is the social network we all depend on.

Respect for the Word

Isocrates, a Greek philosopher of the fifth century B.C., cited the power of speech in the evolution of civilization. In *Antidosis* he argued for a union of oratory and citizenship. One of his arguments addressed the role of speech in establishing a society:

> For in the other powers which we possess we are in no respect superior to other living creatures; nay, we are inferior to many in

swiftness and in strength and in other resources; but, because there has been implanted in us the power to persuade each other and to make clear to each other whatever we desire, not only have we escaped the life of wild beasts, but we have come together and founded cities and made laws and invented arts; and, generally speaking *There is no institution devised by man which the power of speech has not helped us to establish.*[19][italics ours]

Given this, it is small wonder that the respect for the word would be prized by an active and thoughtful statesman such as former Secretary General of the United Nations Dag Hammarskjold, who found himself at the center of global interactions and worried about what he saw.

Hammarskjold wrote about the viability of "the word" in his insightful book *Markings*:

> Respect for the word is the first commandment in the discipline by which a [person] can be educated to maturity—intellectual, emotional, and moral.
>
> Respect for the word—to employ it with scrupulous care and incorruptible heartfelt love of truth—is essential if there is to be any growth in society or in the human race.
>
> To misuse the word is to show contempt for [humanity]. It undermines the bridges and poisons the wells. It causes Man to regress down the long path of his evolution.[20]

This perspective underscores the importance of truthfulness in holding society together and maintaining its quality. Truthfulness is needed to tie together diverse but interdependent people.

This idea is further reinforced by Sissela Bok:

> I can have different kinds of trust: that you will treat me fairly, that you will have my interests at heart, that you will do me no harm. But if I do not trust your word, can I have genuine trust in the first three? If there is no confidence in the truthfulness of others, is there any way to assess their fairness, their intentions to help or to harm? How, then, can they be trusted? *Whatever* matters to human beings, trust is the atmosphere in which it thrives.[21]

Thus it must be acknowledged that truthfulness is among the central virtues. Without it, one can have little assurance of other virtues, such as trustworthiness, fair-mindedness, and benevolence.

Participatory Democracy: Significant Choice and Respect for People

As Peter Winch points out, truthfulness is regarded as a virtue in any viable society but its particular significance in a society can manifest itself in varied ways. For example, the role of citizen participation in decisions on social and political matters varies from society to society. In the United States, participatory democracy can be found in all levels of government, in community affairs, in schools, and even in business and professional life. Although citizens often disagree about the extent to which participatory democracy is (and should be) present in various social and political institutions, it is a valued ideal in our society.

A requirement for effective involvement is that individuals get enough information to permit rational decision making. Thomas Nilsen argues for the need for "significant choice." As he puts it: "The ethical touchstone is the degree of free, informed, rational and critical choice—significant choice—that is fostered by our speaking."[22] Informed choice can be enhanced by various forms of communication—for example, by discussion, dissent, debate, persuasion, and social action. None will be of much value, however, unless the articulation of ideas is based on truthful information.

Significant choice is considered a right by most people in our society. People react with hostility when they perceive that secrecy, limiting access to information, deception, fogging of issues, or half-truths are being intentionally used to interfere with rational decision making. Events in Vietnam and Cambodia, the Watergate cover-up, and the more recent Iran-Contra controversy are illustrations of situations about which many Americans felt that they were deceived by their government, thus limiting their significant choice.

The right to significant choice need not be viewed simply as having social and political value. It can also be regarded as an important element of respect for individuals. This respect typically requires treating people as rational human beings with aims and purposes of their own, about which they are capable of making significant choices. (We say "typically" because many would argue that there are human beings with severely limited rational capacities who are nevertheless entitled to being treated with respect.) Interference with autonomy (or self-determination), whether through physical restraint, deprivation of information, or the use of deception, must be justified. If important information is withheld, distorted, or simply untrue, the ability to exercise significant choice is likely to be impaired. And because people feel that they should be treated decently, they are apt to feel resentment when deceived, even if they would not have decided differently had they been given more truthful information. Although there is a sense in which their autonomy is not undermined in such situations, the lack of respect for their autonomy is evident.

Intimate, Interpersonal Communication

So far in this chapter we have concentrated on communication situations in which speaker and listener do not stand in any special relation to one another. Additional factors come into play in interpersonal communication between friends and loved ones. The poet Adrienne Rich remarks:

> We assume that politicians are without honor. We read their statements trying to crack the code. The scandals of their politics: not that men in high places lie, only that they do so with such indifference, so endlessly, still expecting to be believed. We are accustomed to the contempt inherent in the political lie.
>
> To discover that one has been lied to in a personal relationship, however, leads one to feel a little crazy.[23]

Why, asks Rich, do we feel "a little crazy" when we discover we have been lied to by someone close to us? Her answer points out how much our understanding of even seemingly insignificant events is bound up with the trust we place in those close to us:

> We take so much of the universe on trust. You tell me: "In 1950 I lived on the north side of Beacon Street in Somerville." You tell me: "She and I were lovers, but for months now we have only been good friends." You tell me: "It is seventy degrees outside and the sun is shining." Because I love you, because there is not even a question of lying between us, I take these accounts of the universe on trust: your address twenty-five years ago, your relationship with someone I know only by sight, this morning's weather. I fling unconscious tendrils of belief, like slender green threads, across statements such as these, statements made so unequivocally, which have no tone or shadow of tentativeness. I build them into the mosaic of my world. I allow my universe to change in minute, significant ways, on the basis of things you have said to me, of my trust in you.
>
> I also have faith that you are telling me things it is important I should know; that you do not conceal facts from me in a effort to spare me, or yourself, pain.
>
> Or, at the very least, that you will say, "There are things I am not telling you."

> When we discover that someone we trusted can be trusted no longer, it forces us to reexamine the universe, to question the whole instinct and concept of trust. For a while, we are thrust back onto some bleak, jutting ledge, in a dark pierced by sheets of fire, swept by sheets of rain, in a world before kinship, or naming, or tenderness exist; we are brought close to formlessness.[24]

Rich's probing reflections remind us of how deeply disturbing and disorienting being lied to by someone close to us can be. She points out the fundamental differences between how we communicate with those with whom we have close relationships and others. But should these differences make a *moral* difference? Thomas Nilsen's answer is that they can, although he points out that this possibility may often be overlooked. He suggests the key difference is that the impact of one personality on another is more direct and immediate in close relationships:

> It is in such communications that we most fully share the human condition. The personality is served by speech [that] preserves the dignity and integrity of the individual ego, [that] makes possible the optimum sharing of thought and feeling, the experience of belonging and acceptance, and [that] fosters cooperation and mutual respect. If these aspects of interpersonal communication are not ordinarily thought of as having a significant ethical component, it is because we have lacked a sufficiently inclusive sense of moral obligation.[25]

We prefer to talk about a more inclusive sense of moral responsibility rather than a more inclusive sense of moral obligation. Moral obligation is ordinarily understood in terms of some rather specific moral demands or claims, and it may encourage an excessively legalistic understanding of moral relationships. The idea of moral responsibility includes, but is not necessarily restricted to, duties, obligations, rights, and justice.

One reason thinking clearly about the ethical dimensions of close, interpersonal relationships may be difficult is that, as Nilsen suggests, our understanding of ethics may be too narrowly bound up with notions of duty or obligation. Matters are complicated by the fact that desire and duty or obligation are often thought to be in conflict. One mark of a good relationship is that it is characterized more by a genuine desire to be cooperative, supportive, and caring than by a sense of duty or obligation. One sign of waning friendship or love is that the relationship is defined more and more in terms of rights, duties, obligation, and justice—that genuine caring is becoming replaced by quasi-legalist concerns.

No doubt some depictions of relationships in ethical terms are unattractive. For example, a fundamental difference exists between Alex, who doesn't enjoy playing with his child but does so primarily because he knows that it is a parental duty, and Charles, who genuinely enjoys playing with his child. (Ironically, Charles may come much closer to meeting his parental duties than Alex.)

One might be tempted to conclude from this example that at least in some close relationships, moral or ethical considerations have no place. However, this conclusion would be premature. Admittedly, for a father to play with his child from a sense of duty is less desirable than for him to do so because he genuinely enjoys it—particularly if, as is likely, the child will benefit more from the latter. But Charles can surely be aware that he has parental duties to his child and that playing with her contributes to fulfilling them. Furthermore, he may sometimes decide to forgo other things because he thinks he should play with his child. His friends might try to persuade him to play another set of tennis, which he would enjoy very much. But he may reply: "I'd really like to, but Amy would really be disappointed if I came home late today."

How should we characterize Charles's decision not to play another set of tennis? It could be that although he wants to play another set, he wants to play with Amy even more. It could be that he had promised Amy he would play with her at a certain time. Or it could be that Amy regularly expects Charles to play with her at that time. Any of these reasons seem to be to Charles's credit as a morally sensitive and responsible parent.

Our point is that moral sensitivity and responsibility can be manifested in a variety of ways, only some of which involve acting or refraining from acting primarily because of a concern to do one's duty. Thomas Nilsen's concern, which we share, is that we not overlook those dimensions of close, interpersonal communication that morally call for special sensitivity.

Climate

The kind of climate that two people create in intimate communication is vital to the relationship. A climate of concern, warmth, acceptance, support, and trust is the ideal—trust that the other has our best interests at heart; that the other will not knowingly betray us or let us down; that one can confide in the other; that the other will keep his or her word; that the other is being honest and truthful. In such relationships, trust builds on trust. It is in such a climate that another observation by Nilsen is particularly important to bear in mind: "Whatever improves, develops, enlarges, or enhances human personalities is good; whatever restricts, degrades, or injures human personalities is bad."[26] As Nilsen points out, it is especially in close relationships that our communication can have a profound impact on the growth or diminution of personalities. To illustrate what he has in mind,

Nilsen asks us to imagine a mother standing in her clean living room, waiting for the members of her bridge club to arrive. At that very moment her toddler appears with a wiggling night crawler cupped in his muddy hands. "Look, Mommy, I caught a worm!" he cries out. The mother could respond quite negatively: "Get that worm out of here and go wash your dirty hands." Nilsen asks us to consider the effect this kind of response might have on the child, who undoubtedly is full of enthusiasm and wants to share an exciting experience with his mother.

We may be uncertain about what would be best for both the child and his mother in this situation. Nilsen's point, however, is that the mother does have a moral responsibility to consider the impact a harsh response might have on her child. This example illustrates the special vulnerability one has in close relationships with others. Sensitivity to this vulnerability is a special, and sometimes difficult and demanding, responsibility for those in such relationships.

The child's reaction to a harsh response from his mother might be to *distrust* her in the future. Distrust generates doubts about the integrity, and therefore the reliability, of the other. Sidney Jourard says that the lover's balm is the hater's bomb.[27] Information can be used against a trusting lover by a malicious other. So without trust, we hold back. Once burned, people tend to withhold significant matters until trust is restored.

Discussion Questions

1. Do you agree that truthfulness is necessary as a social norm in order for communication to occur? If so, what responsibilities should communicators accept to encourage effective communication?

2. To what extent do you agree that receivers are coparticipants in the persuasion process? What are the ethical responsibilities of speakers and listeners in a given communication situation? How much responsibility should a receiver accept in being duped by a speaker? What about nonparticipants?

3. Discuss the value of "significant choice" as it relates to listeners in various communication situations.

4. What should speakers do to increase the possibility that listeners will be given "significant choice"? What should listeners do to increase that possibility?

5. What kinds of persuasion do you consider the most ethical? The most unethical? What kinds of interpersonal communication do you consider the most ethical? The most unethical?

6. To what exent do you agree with Nilsen that "Whatever improves, enlarges, or enhances human personalities is good; whatever restricts, degrades, or injures human personalities is bad"? Can we take this dictum too far? Can we not take it far enough? Discuss.

7. What communication values do you believe to be important in an intimate relationship as contrasted with ordinary social relationships? Does the particular relationship with "the other" determine one's responsibility to the other?

8. What is meant by "respect for people"? How might a speaker communicate who shows this respect? How might a speaker communicate who does not show it?

9. How are "significant choice" and "respect for people" linked to the principles of the democratic process? How serious do you consider the harm that has occurred as a result of events such as Vietnam, Watergate, and the Iran-Contra affair? Have other recent events harmed the democratic process?

Public Speaking 101

Jennifer is presenting a persuasive speech in Public Speaking 101 class. She is advocating student action on a matter that has high student interest on campus. You are one of her classmates and are appalled at the inaccuracy of her claims. It is evident to you—but apparently not to the majority of your classmates—that Jennifer has not adequately researched her topic. Unfortunately, she seems to be getting an enthusiastic response from the class anyway. You wonder what you should or should not do. Should you strongly and vehemently indicate your displeasure at these inaccurate and unsupported claims? Should you tell Jennifer that she could have easily acquired the facts had she made the least effort? Should you tell the members of the class that they should be more critical listeners? Should you demand equal time to set them straight? Or should you say nothing, hoping that no harm will come from the speech?

Would it make any difference to you if you knew that Jennifer had high anxiety and low self-esteem? (Or if you knew she had low anxiety and high self-esteem?) Would it matter to you if you knew that Jennifer was very popular with the class and that your critical response would very likely be rejected by the members of the class?

In general, what do you think are your ethical obligations in listening, as well as in speaking, in communication classes?

The Board Listener

Tension grips the room. Union High School is in the middle of a faculty strike. Faculty members have come to a board of trustees meeting to air their concerns. Ms. Speakes, a communication teacher in the school, is listening to the presentations being made by her colleagues. To her dismay, she notices that one of the members of the board is engaging in a good deal of hostile nonverbal behavior. He smiles, smirks, shakes his head in dis-gust, and refuses to look in the direction of faculty speakers.

Speakes decides to confront the board member after the meeting. She approaches him and says firmly but politely, "Mr. Hostelle, I'm sorry, but I was really bothered by your unfriendly behavior during the presentations. Can't you at least *listen* to us?"

Hostelle smiles and says (coolly), "You must have misread me. I was listening." He then walks away, refuses to engage in further dialog, and strikes up a conversation with one of his friends about his son's recent achievements on the football field.

Speakes decides further conversation is hopeless.

Discuss the ethical dimensions of what took place in this situation.

The Selling of the President, 1968

Campaign advisers for Richard M. Nixon were facing a problem: his public image. They wondered how they might positively promote their candidate through television advertising. Harry Treleaven, creative director of advertising in the Nixon campaign, thought he had a solution.

Treleaven decided to make still photography the basis of Nixon's 60-second television commercials. He thought that stills would be perfect for the ads because Nixon himself would not have to appear on the screen. As Joe McGinniss put it in his book *The Selling of the President 1968*:

> Treleaven could use Nixon's voice to accompany the stills but his face would not be on the screen. Instead there would be pictures, and hopefully the pictures would prevent people from paying too much attention to the words. The words would be the same ones Nixon always used— the words of the acceptance speech. But they would all seem fresh and lively because a series of still pictures would flash on the screen while Nixon spoke. If it were done right, it would permit Treleaven to create a Nixon image that was entirely independent of the words. Nixon would say the same old tiresome things but no one would have to listen. The words would become Muzak.

Something pleasant and lulling in the background. The flashing pictures would be carefully selected to create the impression that somehow Nixon represented competence, respect for tradition, serenity, faith that the American people were better than people anywhere else, and that all these problems others shouted about meant nothing in a land blessed with the tallest buildings, strongest armies, biggest factories, cutest children, and rosiest sunsets in the world. Even better: through association with the pictures, Richard Nixon could *become* these very things.[28]

The Nixon advertising campaign apparently was successful, as Nixon won the election. We profess to believe in a democratic form of government in which people have the ultimate say, through the ballot box. We say that we prefer that our votes be based on some degree of informed, rational thought. Yet we seem knowingly to permit, and perhaps even encourage, political campaigns to use the slickest, most manipulative, nonrational means in helping us to determine how we will vote.

Do you think that the persuasive tactics used in the Nixon television campaign are morally acceptable? Discuss.

A Question of Identity

A hospital attendant, Walter, became a father and a widower almost simultaneously when his wife died shortly after giving birth to a son, named Randy. The following year, Walter met Anita, a nurse, who had undergone a hysterectomy. Walter and Anita decided that marriage would work well for them. It would give her a son, which she wanted and could not have naturally, and she would provide the baby with a mother. Walter and Anita decided not to reveal the identity of Randy's natural mother to him and asked family members to cooperate. They felt that it would be better for the child to grow up in a "normal" family situation. As far as Randy knew, his grandparents, two aunts, and an uncle in California were his blood relatives.

For years, Randy never had the slightest reason to suspect that Anita was not his natural mother—especially considering how often women at their church would comment about how much Anita and Randy looked alike. But he remembered that anytime that he would inquire about why he was born in a different city, his father and mother would evade the question, mumbling something and changing the subject. Randy had always wanted a brother—he even prayed for one regularly. When he would ask why he didn't have a brother or sister, his parents would evade this question too, saying that "one child is enough."

When, at age 16, Randy began driver's training, his teacher informed him that he would need to bring his birth certificate to school in order to receive a driver's permit. Randy had never seen his birth certificate (nor had it ever occurred to him to want to see it). He approached his father. "Dad, I need my birth certificate so I can get my driver's permit."

"What are you talking about, Randy?"

"I need the certificate for my permit."

"No you don't. I'll talk to your teacher myself."

Over the next few days, every time Randy asked about his birth certificate, he was given a different answer: "It was burned." "It's lost." "You never had a certificate."

After Randy persisted and threatened to go to the county building to get a copy of the birth certificate, his father reluctantly showed it to him. He explained the identity of Randy's natural mother and relatives on her side of the family.

His father told him how he had met his first wife and married her. She became pregnant, gave birth to Randy, and died a month later from tuberculosis. But after reading the birth certificate more closely, Randy saw that he had a brother. His father explained that this was Randy's stepbrother. Randy's mother had another son in a previous marriage. The discovery that he had the brother he had so badly wanted all of these years somewhat eased the pain Randy felt in discovering that Anita was not his real mother.

As the months passed, however, he found it increasingly difficult to talk to his stepmother. The word *mother* began to stick in his throat. Randy felt that his whole way of thinking had to change. He developed neck cramps from the tension he felt.

Because of the "lie" about the identity of his mother, Randy began to question his father's explanation about everything. Was his mother still alive? Why would his father cut off communication with his mother's family for 16 years? Why didn't his mother's family contact him? Was his father his real father? He even searched his father's personal papers, looking for anything from the past. He came across a marriage license that revealed that his father and his mother were married in May. Randy was born that August. After questioning his father, he discovered that his parents had married to avoid his being born out of wedlock.

At this point Randy had lost so much trust in his father that he sought out more information about his natural mother. He went to various city agencies, but they were unable to help because she had died in another city. He discovered the location of the hospital where she had died. Officials there told him that his mother had died of sickle cell anemia, aggravated by tuberculosis.

Two years later, Randy found out that his brother, Jerry, lived with his grandmother and uncle only a mile away. He was excited about meeting his brother and relatives on his mother's side of the family. His father refused to explain why there had been no communication with them all these years. And Randy could not understand why his relatives had not tried to find him. Neither would accept the responsibility for trying to resolve the situation. Randy's grandmother told him that the family had had no idea where his "crazy" father had taken

him. His father said that it was Randy's relatives who should have taken the initiative to find him. Neither explanation satisfied Randy.

Randy began to get better acquainted with his brother and started bringing him home. His brother complained that he was getting "bad vibes" from Randy's stepmother. Randy's father claimed that she didn't like the idea of having Jerry around because it would remind Walter of his "other family," thus leaving no room for her family. She denied this, and stated "I just want Randy to get to know his family." The mixed signals became so frustrating that Randy began to hate the whole idea of a family.

The consequences:

- Randy no longer talks with any of his natural mother's family, except for his brother (and that was after many stormy arguments and periods of silence).

- His brother, Jerry, often tells him how their grandmother wants him to come by, but Randy feels that had she cared for him, she would have sought him out years ago.

- Walter and Anita have divorced, which may have been partially a result of the conflict over the identity of Randy's real mother.

- Randy does not talk with his father and does not plan to talk with him in the future. He feels that his father does not respect him as a human being.

- His father now feels that maybe he should have told Randy the truth of his mother's identity from the beginning. Randy and Jerry could have grown up together.

• Jerry feels that "what is in the past is in the past." He is very fond of Randy and realizes that he has to make a special effort in the relationship because of Randy's bitterness.[29]

Discussion Questions

1. Was there any acceptable justification for withholding the identity of Randy's mother from him?
2. Should school officials have cooperated with Randy's father in order to conceal the identity of Randy's natural mother?
3. Of what significance was it to Randy that his natural mother had died of sickle cell anemia, aggravated by tuberculosis, rather than tuberculosis alone, as Randy's father had told him?
4. Was there any acceptable justification for withholding from Randy that he had a stepbrother and other relatives living only a mile from his home?
5. How acceptable were the reasons that Randy's relatives on his natural mother's side of the family gave as to why they failed to seek him out?
6. Distinguish between lies, deception, withholding information, and secrets in this case. What other principles of ethical communication appear to have been violated?

Caught in the Middle

Curt and Sherrie are married and in their mid-30s. Curt has a job and Sherrie is a homemaker. They have two children.

Ted is a best friend of both Curt and Sherrie.

While shopping at the mall, Ted and Sherrie run into each other. They haven't talked together for some time, so they decide to have lunch to catch up. Among other things that come up in their conversation, Sherrie tells Ted "the big news." Curt has been offered what she describes as a "simply fantastic job" on the East Coast. It's a "once-in-a-lifetime opportunity," she says. She adds, "If he doesn't take the job, he may never have the chance again. We're both very excited about the opportunity."

Some potential problems loom, however. Curt loves the East, but Sherrie's heart is on the West Coast, where they have lived their entire lives. She is very close to her family, who live nearby, and she still sees old high school friends who live in the area. In addition, she is deeply involved in several community organizations that are quite meaningful to her.

Sherrie tells Ted that she knows this is the kind of opportunity Curt would normally jump at. She says that for some reason, however, he is holding back a little. She thinks his hesitation is based on his loyalty to her and the children. "He's so sweet," says Sherrie. "He wants that job so badly, but he knows my roots are here and that I would probably have some problems adjusting to the East Coast. He knows how important my family and friends are to me—and he knows that it will be a difficult adjustment for the children, too. But I don't want to hold him back. I know he'll be very happy in his new position. So I'm willing to make the sacrifices."

Ted is faced with a dilemma. He knows the real reason Curt is hesitating. Curt has recently confided in him. Although Curt wants to accept the new position, it is his relationship with Sherrie that is holding him back. He is fond of her and committed to his children's welfare. But he is no longer in love with Sherrie. He is certain that problems will develop in their marriage sooner or later, but he cannot reveal his feelings to Sherrie. Ted recalls Curt saying, "It would just shatter Sherrie if she knew how I really feel about her. I think that separation or divorce is in the cards, but I just can't tell her right now how I feel."

What should Ted tell Sherrie? She has asked his advice, saying: "Ted, tell me what you think of all this. What do you think is going on? Can't you convince Curt to take the job? The children and I will be able to handle it." After confiding in Ted, Curt's parting words were, "Ted, please don't say a word to Sherrie about this."

Selected Readings

Argumentation and Persuasion

Andersen, Kenneth E. *Persuasion: Theory and Practice*. 2nd ed. Boston: Allyn and Bacon, 1978. Emphasizes the coactive nature of persuasion. Advocates persuasion that unites people. Source and receiver responsibilities are discussed. Includes a chapter on ethics and persuasion.

Anderson, Jerry M., and Paul Dovre, eds. *Readings in Argumentation*. Boston: Allyn and Bacon, 1968. Contains readings on the ethical duties of the advocate, freedom of speech and debate, rhetoric and philosophical argumentation, logical fallacies, among many well-known contributions in argumentation and debate.

Brembeck, Winston L., and William S. Howell. *Persuasion: A Means of Social Control*. Englewood Cliffs, N.J.: Prentice-Hall, 1952. For many years a standard text in persuasive speaking courses, this book discusses various approaches to the study of ethics in persuasion. The authors advocate the standard of social utility as a means of evaluating persuasion.

Christians, Clifford, Kim Rotzell, and Mark Fackler. *Media Ethics*. 2nd ed. New York: Longman, 1987. A good case study book in media ethics, including journalism, public relations, advertising, and broadcasting. Presents a methodology to aid in the analysis of a variety of cases.

Haiman, Franklyn S. *Freedom of Speech: Issues and Cases*. New York: Random House, 1965. A book that grew out of the establishment of the Committee on Freedom of Speech in the Speech Communication Association. Presents cases for analysis on issues central to the study of ethics and freedom of speech.

Jensen, J. Vernon. *Argumentation: Reasoning in Communication*. Belmont, Calif.: Wadsworth, 1981. Firmly grounded in the values of argumentation and debate in society. Emphasizes the ethical responsibilities of speakers to both the immediate and not-immediate audience. Written within the liberal arts tradition.

Johannesen, Richard L., ed. *Ethics and Persuasion: Selected Readings*. New York: Random House, 1967. A central source book of a variety of readings that explore ethical problems relative to persuasion. Readings analyze ethical issues, democratic premises, philosophical perspectives, and ethical problems in mass persuasion.

Larson, Charles U. *Persuasion: Reception and Responsibility*. Belmont, Calif.: Wadsworth, 1986. This contemporary book in persuasion develops a receiver-oriented approach. Heavily influenced by the writings of the rhetorical philosopher Richard Weaver. Features a major chapter by Richard L. Johannesen on a variety of ethical perspectives in persuasion.

Minnick, Wayne C. *The Art of Persuasion*. Boston: Houghton Mifflin, 1968. Includes a chapter on the ethics of persuasion that analyzes various treatments of ends and means. The author advocates a "middle ground" position.

O'Donnell, Victoria, and June Kable. *Persuasion: An Interactive Dependency Approach*. New York: Random House, 1982. A transactional view of communication. Considers persuasion as a reciprocal activity where the interdependent participants influence one another. Emphasis is on both the persuader and the persuadee. Responsibility is a shared value.

Simons, Herbert W. *Persuasion: Understanding, Practice, and Analysis.* 2nd ed. New York: Random House, 1976. Written from a coactive approach to persuasion. Mutual responsibilities of receivers and speakers are implicit. The author addresses some of the ethical ironies of what is expected from speakers and what often happens in the persuasive situation.

Smith, Mary John. *Persuasion and Human Action: A Review and Critique of Social Influence Theories.* Belmont, Calif.: Wadsworth, 1982. The dominant focus is on what people intentionally "do with" persuasive message, not what messages "do to" people. People are viewed as active agents, having the capacity for choice and self-direction. The approach has significant implications for ethical responsibilities of coacting communicators.

Sproule, J. Michael. *Argument: Language and Its Influence.* New York: McGraw-Hill, 1980. A substantial chapter on the ethics of argument and persuasion is included. An analysis of media and advertising ethics, codes of ethics, and principles of ethics.

Rhetoric, Rhetorical Criticism, and Public Address

The Rhetoric of Aristotle. Translated by Lane Cooper. New York: Appleton-Century-Crofts, 1932. All three books of Aristotle's *Rhetoric* are included, preceded by a synthesis, interpretation, and evaluation of the importance of the work. A classic.

Baird, A. Craig. *American Public Addresses: 1740–1952.* Vol. 1. New York: McGraw-Hill, 1956. A collection of speeches by 26 speakers including clergy, lawyers, teachers, members of Congress, presidents, politicians, popular lecturers, journalists, labor leaders. Brief introductions set the scene for each speech.

Blankenship, Jane. *Public Speaking: A Rhetorical Perspective.* Englewood Cliffs, N.J.: Prentice-Hall, 1966. A public speaking text that synthesizes speech principles based on classical and contemporary rhetorical theory. Contains two chapters on rhetorical invention, including a discussion of ethical proof.

Bosmajian, Haig A., ed. *Readings in Speech.* New York: Harper & Row, 1965. Contains a number of readings in rhetoric, propaganda, democratic ethics, totalitarianism, character of the speaker. Includes some well-known speeches.

Graham, John. *Great American Speeches.* New York: Appleton-Century-Crofts, 1970. Twenty-four 20th-century speeches and a dozen studies of earlier periods of American public address. A number of the speeches can be studied for the ethical values they represent.

Hochmuth, Marie, ed. *A History and Criticism of American Public Address.* Vol. 3. New York: Longmans, Green, 1955. The third in a series of studies under the auspices of the Speech Association of America. Eleven studies of speakers. Includes an essay on "The Criticism of Rhetoric" by the editor.

Linkugel, Wil A., R. R. Allen and Richard L. Johannesen. *Contemporary American Speeches: A Sourcebook of Speech Forms and Principles.* Belmont, Calif.: Wadsworth, 1965. Uses the analysis of speeches to study principles of effective speaking. Includes seven speeches that affirm various propositions of value. Contains an index of rhetorical principles, referring directly to their use in the text of the speeches.

McBurney, James H., James M. O'Neill and Glen E. Mills. *Argumentation and Debate: Techniques of a Free Society.* New York: Macmillian, 1951. An influential book in the field of argumentation and debate. Provides a treatment representative of a number of books that followed over several years.

Nilsen, Thomas R., ed. *Essays on Rhetorical Criticism.* New York: Random House, 1968. Includes contributions by major scholars in rhetorical criticism. Provides the student interested in ethics with important perspectives that can be applied to ethical criticism.

Ross, Raymond S. *Speech Communication: Fundamentals and Practice.* Englewood Cliffs, N.J.: Prentice-Hall, 1983. A well-known text in the fundamentals of speech communication. Emphasizes the ethics and responsibilities of both speakers and receivers. Discusses source credibility, ethical proof, and impression management as fundamental considerations for persuasion.

Scott, Robert L., and Bernard L. Brock. *Methods of Rhetorical Criticism: A Twentieth-Century Perspective.* New York: Harper & Row, 1972. A contemporary book in rhetorical criticism. The authors identify an emerging issue regarding ethical evaluation in their introduction. Provides a substantial treatment of rhetorical criticism by the authors and a variety of scholars.

Thompson, Wayne N. *Responsible and Effective Communication.* Boston: Houghton Mifflin, 1978. The entire book is written from a perspective that communicators should be responsible. Chapter 1 discusses the ethics of communication. Remaining chapters attempt to develop the responsible and effective communicator.

Thonssen, Lester, and A. Craig Baird. *Speech Criticism.* New York: Ronald Press, 1948. A classic in the field of speech criticism. Nature of rhetorical criticism, development of rhetorical theory, methods of the critics, standards of judgment are all discussed. The integrity of ideas and the integrity of speakers are emphasized. A chapter on the character of the speaker.

Weaver, Richard. *The Ethics of Rhetoric.* Chicago: Regnery, 1953. A philosophical treatise. Explores the attitudes exhibited by the neutral speaker, the evil speaker, and the noble speaker. Intrinsic qualities of ethical communication and the view of the speaker toward the audience receive comprehensive discussion.

Wilson, John F., and Carroll C. Arnold. *Public Speaking as a Liberal Art.* Boston: Allyn and Bacon, 1964. A basic book in public speaking. Written from a liberal arts perspective. Provides a good deal of discussion of rhetoric, including an exposition of the richness of classical contributions to the development of ethical traditions.

Interpersonal Communication

Arnett, Ronald C. *Communication and Community.* Carbondale: Southern Illinois Press, 1986.

————. *Dwell in Peace: Applying Nonviolence to Everyday Relationships.* Elgin, Ill.: Brethren Press, 1985. These two books emphasize humanistic communication. Ethics permeates Arnett's works, especially from the perspective that the kind of communication we engage in shapes the nature of our world. Arnett's interpretative work on Buber makes it clear that Buber did not confine himself only to one-to-one relationships.

Brown, Charles T., and Paul W. Keller. *Monologue to Dialogue: An Exploration of Interpersonal Communication.* 2nd ed. Englewood Cliffs, N.J.: Prentice-Hall, 1979. Emphasizes the importance of dialog in communication. Chapter 11 expands an earlier article by Keller and Brown, "An Interpersonal Ethic for Communication," *Journal of Communication* 18 (March 1968): 73–81. The authors say that dialog is ethical if the speaker accepts the listener, even if the speaker disagrees with the positions taken by the listener. The self-determining forces of individuals should be enhanced in dialog.

Buber, Martin. *1-and-Thou.* 2nd ed. Translated by Ronald Gregor Smith. New York: Scribners, 1958.

———. *The Knowledge of Man.* Edited with an introduction by Maurice Friedman. New York: Harper & Row, 1965. Two major works of Buber that are relevant to communication as dialog. Buber's writings have ethical implications because of his belief that "I-and-Thou" relationships are what makes us human. He identifies the characteristics of "I-and-Thou" dialog.

Condon, John. *Interpersonal Communication.* New York: Macmillan, 1977. Considers ethics as a responsibility in interpersonal communication. Chapter 8 addresses several variables in ethical communication: candor, social harmony, fidelity, deception, acknowledgments, consistency of word and act, keeping confidences, sharing, access to secrets, and invasions of privacy.

Devito, Joseph A. *The Interpersonal Communication Book.* 3rd ed. New York: Harper & Row, 1983. Presents ethics in a prominent position (one of four preliminaries to interpersonal communication). Topics include ethical bases, an ethic for listening, choice, lying, fear and emotional appeals, and prevention of interaction.

Fromm, Erich. *The Art of Loving.* New York: Harper & Row, 1963. Several elements of the art of loving are discussed. They include giving, care, responsibility, respect, and knowledge. Fromm perceives that love finds major expression in communication with others and that oneness is one of the most exhilarating and exciting experiences in life.

Howell, William S. *The Empathic Communicator.* Belmont, Calif.: Wadsworth, 1982. Howell emphasizes the need for communicators to be empathic. He discusses his operational perspective on ethics in chapter 8. He is interested in culturally and interculturally derived ethical values and believes that we should consider whether ethics works in society.

Johannesen, Richard L. *Ethics in Human Communication.* 2nd ed. Prospect Heights, Ill.: Waveland Press, 1983. A particularly useful resource for students of communication ethics. Provides a comprehensive survey of issues in communication ethics and theories of ethics and values that can be used to analyze those issues.

Jourard, Sidney. *The Transparent Self.* Princeton, N.J.: Van Nostrand, 1964. A classic work in self-disclosing communication. Jourard takes the position that we can know "who we are" only through communication with another significant person. He agrees with Buber that we function at our most human level in "I-and-Thou" relationships.

Mayeroff, Milton. *On Caring.* Evanston: Harper & Row, Perennial Library, 1971. Succinctly written with significant meanings. The major ingredients of caring are explained. An ethic of care is implicit.

Nilsen, Thomas. *Ethics of Speech Communication*. 2nd ed. Indianapolis: Bobbs-Merrill, 1974. Nilsen emphasizes the need for significant choice in communication. Interpersonal communication is seen to have special characteristics that require considerations unnecessary in public communication situations. Self-determination and personal growth have ethical implications in communication.

Rogers, Carl. *On Becoming a Person*. Boston: Houghton Mifflin, 1961. A classic discussion on the importance of empathy in communication. Elements of helping relationships are discussed.

Schutz, William C. *Joy*. New York: Grove Press, 1967. Basic human needs are discussed: the need for inclusion, affection, and control. These may be seen as having ethical implications in human encounters.

Stewart, John. *Bridges Not Walls*. 4th ed. New York: Random House, 1986. Develops the thesis that the quality of a person's life is directly related to the quality of the communication he or she experiences. The metaphor of the "spiritual child" is used to explain the creation of particular relationships.

Weaver, Richard. *Understanding Interpersonal Communication*. 3rd ed. Glenview, Ill.: Scott, Foresman, 1986. An introductory text in interpersonal communication. Provides a view of many important concepts relating to self-disclosure and listening.

Wilmot, William. *Dyadic Communication: A Transactional Perspective*. Menlo Park, Calif.: Addison-Wesley, 1975. Written exclusively from a two-person perspective. Intimacy and dyadic relationships are emphasized. Helpful from the perspective of focusing on one-to-one communication.

METHODS OF REASONING IN ETHICS

MORAL REASONING

So far, about morals, I know only that what is moral is what you feel good after and what is immoral is what you feel bad after and judged by these moral standards, which I do not defend, the bullfight is very moral to me because I feel very fine while it is going on and have a feeling of life and death and mortality and immortality, and after it is over I feel very sad but very fine.

—Ernest Hemingway[1]

When Raymond Baumhart interviewed 100 people in business nearly 20 years ago, 50 percent said that what *ethical* means to them is "what my feelings tell me is right."[2] There is little reason to think that they would have answered much differently if *moral* had been substituted for *ethical*. Nor is there much reason to suppose that their responses were unusual, or that much has changed in this regard in the last 20 years. Many people do think of morality as being largely a matter of personal feelings.

However, the passage from Hemingway should make us pause for reflection. Perhaps some would agree with that assessment of bullfighting, although many might wonder why the bull is given no say in the matter. If we were to substitute *war, terrorism, murder, rape*, or *assault* for *bullfight*, most would think that something had gone wrong. Even if a few people feel good about these activities, most of us would resist the idea that we must thereby concede that, for these people, these activities are morally acceptable. "Feeling it's so doesn't make it so," we might object.

Important as feelings are in morality, they do not seem to provide a reliable and consistent guide to moral thinking. Equally important is the use of reason. The relation between reason and feelings in morality is quite complex and probably not fully understood. However, it seems clear that conscience, especially reflective conscience, is not merely a matter of feelings.

In this chapter we will consider some of the typical ways reasoning is used in situations calling for moral judgment. As will be seen, we do not all reason the same way even when confronted with essentially similar circumstances. Not only do we often reason differently from one another, we often, as individuals, vary our own reasoning from situation to situation. Sometimes this variation happens because we realize that different contexts may call for different kinds of reasoning. But sometimes we seem to be suffering from narrow vision, or even inconsistency.

Moral Development

What happens in early childhood clearly has an important bearing on the moral development of human beings. Fear of punishment and fear of the loss of love play a fundamental role in shaping the moral values of very young children. Followers of Sigmund Freud suggest that the development of moral character and habits of moral thought is essentially complete before children even begin their formal education.[3] The die has been cast. Understandably, such a view is disturbing to parents, who fear they may irretrievably fail during their early years of parenting—those years when they are just beginning to figure out what parenting is all about, and when their children's rational capacities are only partially developed. It is also discouraging to educators, who might otherwise have hoped that they could constructively assist their students' moral development as their reasoning abilities develop.

The Freudian view has met considerable resistance, particularly from Lawrence Kohlberg and his followers.[4] Kohlberg conducted extensive research for more than 25 years on the moral development of children and adults. Unlike the Freudians, Kohlberg believes that moral development undergoes significant structural changes well into adulthood. Following the lead of Jean Piaget, Kohlberg stresses the importance of cognitive features of moral development.[5] Moral development in the child involves the gradual adoption of more and more logically sophisticated forms of moral reasoning. This presumably takes place in an invariant, sequential manner.

According to Piaget, children's cognitive capacities develop in stages. For example, very young children can readily observe that one stick is longer than another. If they are presented with two sticks, they can see that stick A is longer than stick B. If A is then hidden from view and B is paired with stick C, which is seen to be shorter than B, these same children will not immediately infer that C is also shorter than A. Instead, they will ask to see A again so that it can be directly compared with C. Somewhat older children can reason hypothetically about something concrete. For example, they will immediately conclude that John is taller than Richard when told that Amy is taller than Richard and John is taller than Amy. However, these same children might not be able to reason abstractly that if A is greater than B and B is greater than C, then A is greater than C.

Variations on such examples present further logical difficulties for children. The same children who readily conclude that John is taller than Richard because Amy is taller than Richard and John is taller than Amy might hesitate when told instead that Richard is shorter than Amy. They may have some difficulty understanding the reciprocal relationship between *taller* and *shorter*.

Such limitations in logical thinking have, according to Piaget and Kohlberg, correlates in the social sphere. Relatively young children might understand elementary reciprocal relations such as exchanging punishment for misdeeds, hitting back, or having to do something for someone else in order to get something in return. More sophisticated, however, is the ability to recognize differences between one's own perspective and that of others (for example, the fact that we do not all like the same things).

The failure to recognize or appreciate the significance of these differences is called *egocentric* thinking. Overcoming, or at least reducing, egocentricity is an essential element of moral development. Unfortunately, it is not only children whose thinking has egocentric shortcomings. Adults, too, have egocentric tendencies, although this often is more a matter of not making the effort to take into account differing perspectives than an inability to do so.

Overcoming egocentricity can involve many different levels of reciprocal awareness. For example, John might notice that Amy is looking at him. But Amy might realize that John has noticed this. In turn, John might suspect that Amy realizes that John has noticed this! And so on. Reciprocal understanding is fundamental to many types of social interaction. It may be instrumental to success in game playing (poker, for example) or in developing social strategies. While it may be used for manipulative and possibly exploitive purposes, reciprocal understanding is also fundamental to developing and maintaining desirable social relationships.[6]

Kohlberg's Stages

Kohlberg's stages of moral development are divided into three levels, each of which contains two stages. The first level is *preconventional thinking*, with a predominantly self-interested orientation. Stage 1 is marked by a fear of punishment or loss of love and the hope for reward. Stage 2 is often characterized as a "back-scratching" stage. This rudimentary form of reciprocity is aptly summarized as "You scratch my back and I'll scratch yours." The motivation is not so much a concern for fairness as a recognition of the need for minimal forms of cooperation in order to get what one wants. None of us is wholly self-sufficient. But assistance from others typically comes only if one is willing to reciprocate. So it is seen that one must keep agreements, do one's part, and the like.

According to Kohlberg, these two stages are predominant among children up to about age nine, but he adds that this preconventional level is characteristic of some adolescents and many adolescent and adult criminal offenders.[7] In addition to being highly self-interested, preconventional moral reasoning is highly egocentric. Young children, especially, have difficulty understanding the perspectives of others and social relationships that depend on reciprocal understanding. The child has a tendency to assume that others see things just the way he or she does. Thus a young child may give a present to an older sibling that is of no real interest to the older child—the younger child mistakenly assumes that the older sibling shares the same interests.

Egocentric behavior might seem to be intentionally self-serving. But it need not be. The younger child might genuinely wish to please the older child but simply not realize what this requires. As the child begins to develop an understanding of the different perspectives of others, he or she can advance to Kohlberg's second level of moral reasoning, *conventional thinking*. Stage 3 (the "good boy, good girl" stage) is based on a genuine concern for others, as expressed in friendship, loyalty, and, especially, the desire for social approval. Someone in stage 3 has to be sensitive to the expectations of others in order to know how to win their acceptance and approval.

Although stage 3 moral reasoning moves beyond the egocentric limitations of stages 1 and 2, it has its own limitations. Stage 3 thinkers tend not to resolve moral issues from the standpoint of social institutions or a systematic legal or social order. According to Kohlberg, stage 3 reasoning falls short particularly in situations where one is called on to mediate between two or more individuals whose interests or desires are in conflict. Stage 4 reasoning, characterized as the "law and order" stage, can help mediate such conflicts by appealing to widely accepted rules or laws.

However, reasoning at Kohlberg's second level, whether at stage 3 or stage 4, remains conventional rather than critical. Both conventional stages are characterized by pressures to conform to commonly accepted moral expectations, standards, or rules. These pressures may come from peers in the form of explicit social approval or disapproval. They may also come from the more subtle pressures that prevail in institutional settings.

("Groupthink" will be discussed in depth in Part Three.) Stage 4 is marked by respect for various types of authority—institutional, governmental, or religious. What is missing, however, is critical evaluation of these sources of authority.

To say that one's thinking or behavior is conventional, or conforming, is not necessarily to say that there is anything wrong with it. For example, clothing styles are conventional, but typically harmless. They might even be desirable. But the acceptability of *moral* conventions is dependent on what those conventions happen to be; it cannot be assumed that everything that is conventionally accepted is morally acceptable. For example, today many of the traditionally accepted roles of men and women are being subjected to moral criticism. The question of whether men and women should have equal opportunities in the workplace cannot be satisfactorily answered by simply citing commonly accepted practices of the past. The same is true of the question of the extent to which household and child-rearing responsibilities should be shared by men and women.

The third level of Kohlberg's theory is *postconventional thinking*. It is marked by *critical reflection* on the types of moral reasoning used in the earlier stages. Kohlberg is convinced that this critical perspective ultimately leads one autonomously to base moral judgments on considerations of universal human rights and respect for human dignity, rather than simply self-interest, concern for friends or loved ones, or regard for some particular social or political structure. This detached perspective does not mean that the latter considerations are rejected as irrelevant; rather, they are considered in relation to each other and to more universal, abstract moral principles. From the developmental standpoint, the most striking contrast between the earlier stages and stages 5 and 6 is that the latter two are self-reflective, and those who reason at this level exhibit greater independence of mind in moral judgment at the same time that they embrace a more comprehensive and impartial point of view.

Although Kohlberg is convinced that advancement from stage to stage moves one closer to accepting principles that respect the rights and dignity of all, he insists that *how* one reasons to a conclusion, rather than the conclusion itself, distinguishes the stages from one another. It is quite possible for opposite conclusions to be drawn from the same type of reasoning. For example, each of the following seems to exemplify stage 2 reasoning. In the musical *Annie*, Daddy Warbucks says: "You don't have to be nice to the people you meet on the way up, if you're not coming back down again." The more cautious John Wooden allegedly told his players after UCLA won the NCAA basketball title in 1964: "Be gracious to those whom you have defeated on the way up to this pinnacle, because you will be meeting those same people on the way down."[8]

Although Kohlberg's theory has attracted many followers, it has some problems. The theory is not just a *descriptive* account of moral development. Built into the theory are certain philosophical assumptions that many consider controversial. Not only does development allegedly take place in an invariant, sequential manner (no stage can be skipped, and no regression to earlier stages takes place), each succeeding stage is claimed to be *more adequate* morally than the preceding ones. However, it is not obvious that later stages in Kohlberg's hierarchical scheme are always preferable to earlier ones.

For example, consider the following *Newsweek* story:

> Nine-year-old Ralph Heard, Jr., didn't think he was a hero for saving his mother and brother from their burning apartment last year. Neither, it appeared, did anyone else in Atlanta. No local paper reported the fire; a neighbor whom Ralph helped rescue sued for damages because the flames had started in the Heard apartment, and when Ralph returned to Kimberley Elementary School after six weeks in an emergency unit (where it was feared that facial burns had blinded him), classmates jeered at his headmask with taunts of "burnt boy."
>
> Ralph came home in tears most days—sobbing as he never had at the burns that seared 50 percent of his body. But eventually justice triumphed, sort of. After Ralph's mother moved the family to a new school district, a visiting fire marshal noticed Ralph's mask and asked for explanations. The story touched off a string of tardy tributes from a local radio station, the Hartford Insurance Group, Atlanta Mayor Maynard Jackson and even the governor—who honored him with a special proclamation in the gold-domed capital.
>
> Still, Ralph hasn't lost sight of the painful surgery ahead or of the painful mockery behind him. "Yes, I'd do it again," he answered a reporter after pondering for several minutes. "But only for my family. Not for nobody else."[9]

What would Kohlberg say of young Ralph's reasoning after his ordeal? Ralph actually risked his life to help save a neighbor, which suggests that Ralph was at least at stage 3 prior to his misfortune. However, now Ralph says that he would do it again, but only for his family. This, in Kohlberg's view, would seem to be moral regression, perhaps to stage 2, where actual reciprocation occurs ("You scratch my back and I'll scratch yours").

But to conclude that Ralph's moral reasoning has regressed seems rather harsh. His heroic efforts resulted in derision by his classmates and a lawsuit on the part of his neighbor. The derision threatened his self-esteem. It seems both reasonable and morally acceptable in such a circumstance to refuse to do again something that might have such consequences. What is especially interesting about this example is that it is Ralph's sensitivity to what his peers think of him (stage 3) that is responsible for his "regression" to stage 2. But rather than revealing a lack of moral maturity, Ralph's response suggests that a problem exists in his social environment. It is not clear that Kohlberg's theory takes into consideration this kind of limitation in social setting.

Ralph's heroics suggest another shortcoming in Kohlberg's theory. The key moral concepts in Kohlberg's theory are impartiality, reciprocity, justice, rights, duties, and individual autonomy and independence. As Carol Gilligan has recently pointed out, compassion, caring, interdependence, responsiveness to needs, and concern for relationships between people receive little attention.[10] Insofar as Kohlberg does consider them, they seem to be relegated to stage 3 rather than the higher stages. Yet it is precisely these concepts that seem best to characterize Ralph's initial concern to help his neighbors and his later concern for family relationships.

Gilligan contends that Kohlberg's theory underestimates the complexity and importance of what she calls a "morality of care." She argues that Kohlberg's account perceives people as quite autonomous and independent and that a theory of moral development should also emphasize compassion, caring, responsibility, and interdependence. She raises some fundamental questions about the ways we approach moral situations. Kohlberg's account emphasizes: Is it right? Is it fair or just? Is it a duty or obligation? Gilligan's account emphasizes: Can I help? Will I hurt someone? What is needed? How will relationships be affected?

We need to ask which of these questions (or others) seem most relevant in communication settings. Certainly there are many situations in which Kohlberg's questions are important to keep in mind. However, Gilligan's are equally important. It is not only questions of justice that need to be considered when we wonder whether we should lie, withhold or volunteer information, protect secrets or confidential matters, advise or not advise others, console or criticize associates, friends, or loved ones, and so on. These issues arise in business and professional settings as well as in more intimate, personal relationships.

Ironically, Kohlberg's famous Heinz example illustrates the limitations of his theory. This example is commonly used by Kohlberg and his associates to determine the level of "justice reasoning" of those being interviewed. Heinz's wife is dying of cancer. He has tried to raise money to buy a drug that might save her, but he has been unsuccessful. The druggist is charging $2,000 for the drug, but Heinz has been able to raise only $1,000, and the druggist is unwilling to advance credit to him. Should Heinz steal the drug to save his wife? Suppose the dying person were a stranger. Should Heinz steal the drug to save the stranger? According to Kohlberg, if Heinz would steal the drug for his wife but not the stranger, his reasoning is at a lower stage than if, out of respect for the right to life, he would steal for either.

But is stealing the drug out of love for his wife really a morally less adequate response than stealing it for his wife out of respect for her right to life? In fact, stealing out of love seems more suitable to a loving relationship. Stealing for a stranger might be morally commendable in some circumstances, but does a person's right to life impose such a duty on Heinz? Stealing for a stranger does not seem to be a requirement of justice. Such an act seems to be "above and beyond the call of duty." It is more appropriately characterized as an act of benevolence grounded in fellow-feeling or compassion, rather than justice and rights. Thus Gilligan's "morality of care" seems more relevant here than Kohlberg's "morality of justice."

Despite its limitations, Kohlberg's theory of moral development has much to offer. First, by describing many common types of moral reasoning, it encourages us to be more reflective about how we typically *do* arrive at our moral judgments. Second, by arranging those types of moral reasoning hierarchically, it encourages us to raise critical questions about how we *should* arrive at our moral judgments. Third, Kohlberg's theory encourages us to be more autonomous, or critical, in our moral thinking. Fourth, it alerts us to our egocentric tendencies and encourages us to develop more consistent and comprehensive habits of moral thought. Finally, by focusing on the importance of giving reasons for our moral judgments, it emphasizes that morality is not just a matter of feelings. Giving reasons in support of our moral judgments is an essential part of attempting to *justify* those judgments. It is to a more detailed discussion of what is involved in moral justification that we will now turn.

Moral Justification

To attempt to morally justify a principle, belief, attitude, policy, or action is to seek good reasons in support of it. Good reasons are reasons one is willing to commend to others rather than simply accept privately. This is what is meant by saying that justificatory processes are essentially public, not private.[11]

It is important to realize that this public requirement does not mean that one is never justified in engaging in deceptive practices or in withholding information from others. For example, consider the question of whether doctors are ever justified in withholding diagnostic information from their patients. Most would concede that although information ordinarily should not be withheld, exceptional cases do occur. If, in such an exceptional case, Dr. Smith is justified in delaying telling Mr. Adams about his condition, this does not mean that Dr. Smith should be willing to announce publicly that she is doing this. Such an announcement would obviously be self-defeating. Rather, Dr. Smith must be willing to defend publicly the idea that in certain *kinds* of situations, withholding information of this sort is justified. That is, she should be willing to acknowledge and defend her acceptance of this kind of practice, but she is not required to announce to all the world that Mr. Adams's circumstance is a case in point.

Universalizability and Reversibility

What moral justification requires is that one's reasons be generalizable to similar situations. More formally, moral judgments must be *universalizable*: Whatever is right (or wrong) in one situation is right (or wrong) in any relevantly similar situation.[12] Essentially, this requirement demands that our moral reasoning be internally consistent. If Dr. Smith is justified in delaying information to Mr. Adams, she is justified in doing the same in any relevantly similar situation. So are other doctors. Furthermore, Dr. Smith must consider whether withholding information in this particular situation is relevantly similar to nonmedical situations in which one is inclined to withhold information from others.

A related requirement of moral justification is that one's judgments be *reversible*.[13] In principle, Dr. Smith will have to acknowledge that relevantly similar situations could arise in which someone would be justified in withholding vital information from her. Thus she must be prepared to ask what she would say if the roles were reversed and she were the patient.

Standards and Circumstances

Clearly, moral justification requires imaginative, consistent, and comprehensive thinking. The quest for justification is an attempt to take into consideration and appropriately weigh all morally relevant factors. Just what those factors are, and how important they are, vary with circumstances and may be a matter of some controversy. In general, however, these factors will be of two sorts: (1) relevant moral standards and principles; and (2) relevant information about the circumstances calling for moral judgment.

Moral standards and principles identify the general kinds of considerations one should bear in mind when making moral judgments. Such considerations include: possible short- and long-term harms and benefits to individuals, groups, interpersonal relationships, social and political institutions and practices, and the environment; respect for people; justice (for example, equality, fairness, and desert); and various rights, obligations, duties, commitments, and responsibilities.

Moral standards and principles must be applied to particular circumstances. So it is also necessary to acquire as much relevant information as one can about these circumstances. Often we do not have all the information we might wish to have before making decisions or recommendations. This may be because we have to decide before we have had enough time to acquire or digest the relevant information. Or it may be that the information simply is not available.

Note also that determinations of fact often cannot be separated from those of value. For example, in attempting to gather information about possible harms and benefits, one already has to have made some value judgments about what counts as a harm or benefit. Everyone would agree that suffering a broken arm in an accident is a harm. What about critically evaluating a sensitive student's oral presentation in front of the rest of the class?

Finally, even if we were all to agree on the moral standards and principles to use as criteria for moral judgment, we may find that these criteria conflict with one another in some circumstances. For example, what is good for a group might be very harmful or unfair to a particular individual, or it might pose a serious threat to his or her fundamental rights.

Given the confusion and perplexity that so often characterize our attempts at moral justification, we might hope for some all-embracing theory to systematically evaluate our moral thinking. Moral philosophers have made many attempts to provide such a theory. We will briefly mention a few.

Moral Theories

One common kind of moral theory is broadly characterized as *consequentialist*. It insists that what really matters morally are good and bad consequences, that the fundamental question to ask when trying to determine whether an act, policy, or practice is right or wrong is, "What good (or ill) is likely to come of it?"

Good or ill for whom? *Egoistic* theories focus on what is good or bad for oneself.[14] The egoist view is that one should seek to maximize good consequences and minimize bad consequences for oneself. This view is popularly summarized: "Looking out for Number One." At the other extreme is *utilitarianism*, which holds that we should attempt to promote the greatest good for the greatest number of individuals.[15] Many utilitarians believe that our concern should extend to all creatures capable of experiencing pleasure or pain, not just human beings.

Between the extremes of egoism and utilitarianism lie many consequentialist variations. Some focus on maximizing good consequences for one's country, one's community, one's business, one's circle of friends and associates, or one's family. Others focus on minimizing harms rather than maximizing good consequences. In any variation, however, the focus is on good or bad consequences.

Another kind of moral theory emphasizes the importance of *nonconsequentialist* features of morality. This kind of theory is sometimes called *deontological*, because of its emphasis on acting on principle and its appeal to rights and duties that are not grounded solely in considerations of good or bad consequences. For example, one might claim that promises should be kept because to make a promise is voluntarily to accept a duty, or obligation, to do something. Of course, the making and keeping of promises often has good consequences. But barring exceptional circumstances (when keeping a promise to meet someone would require one not to help one's ailing child, for example), one should keep his or her promise even if more good might come from breaking it.

The most famous nonconsequentialist, or deontological, theory is that of the 18th-century philosopher Immanuel Kant. Kant's fundamental moral principle is his *categorical imperative*, which insists that we act only on considerations that we would find acceptable for anyone and that respect the dignity of people.[16]

Until quite recently, most contemporary discussions of moral theory have concentrated on standards and principles for evaluating actions, policies, practices, and social and political institutions. Historically, however, moral theories have been equally concerned with matters of *moral character*. This was certainly true of the philosophers of ancient Greece, such as Plato and Aristotle. Theories that emphasize moral character are commonly referred to as *virtue* theories.

Virtue theories cut across the consequentialist-nonconsequentialist divide in moral theory. Virtues such as benevolence and generosity may seem more at home in consequentialist theories, while conscientiousness and the sense of duty may seem more at home in nonconsequentialist theories. However, virtues such as courage and honesty do not seem clearly to lean in one direction rather than the other.

Perhaps the question to be asked is what moral importance should be attached to one's having or not having a given virtue. Those who value virtues only for their social utility, for example, would emphasize consequentialist features of certain virtues. The more deontologically inclined might focus on those virtues that seem to them to be marks of personal integrity (for example, "a person of principle"), quite apart from their social utility.

We will not attempt to settle exclusively on any single moral theory or principle. Our approach to questions of justification is more pluralistic. We find attractive features in all of these basic approaches. In subsequent chapters in Part Two, we will concentrate primarily on questions concerning the justification of lying. No one theory seems to us to have a monopoly on relevant considerations. Although some of our observations may be peculiar to lying, much of what we will say about justification can be applied to other types of communication as well.

Ethical Perspectives of Executives and the Public

In the summer of 1983, the Gallup Organization conducted an ethics survey for the *Wall Street Journal*. A representative national sampling of the general public was taken; 1,558 adults were personally interviewed. In addition, 396 middle-level, big-company executives filled out confidential questionnaires. Gallup estimates that the public poll has a sampling error of up to 3 percent and the executive poll up to 5 percent.

Many of the situations that the public and executives were asked to respond to dealt with communication issues. In fact, all six examples discussed in Roger Ricklefs's November 3 report involved communication problems.[17]

The first case poses a dilemma for an employer who discovers that the best-qualified candidate for a job lied about what he earned at his last job. He earned only $18,000, not the $28,000 he reported. Should the employer hire the candidate anyway, or should he choose someone else (who will be less qualified)? Interestingly, 63 percent of the general public recommended hiring the candidate, despite his lie, whereas only 47 percent of the executives said they would hire such a person. (Only 27 percent of the general public said the employer should choose someone else. However, 52 percent of the executives said they would choose someone else.)

The other five dilemmas, along with the survey results, are presented below.

Family vs. Ethics

Jim, a 56-year-old middle manager with children in college, discovers that the owners of his company are cheating the government out of several thousand dollars a year in taxes. Jim is the only employee who would be in a position to know this. Should Jim report the owners to the Internal Revenue Service at the risk of endangering his own livelihood, or disregard the discovery in order to protect his family's livelihood?

> Survey results: 49 percent of the public and 52 percent of the executives think Jim should disregard his discovery so that he can protect his family. 34 percent of each think Jim should report the owners.

The Roundabout Raise

When Joe asks for a raise, his boss praises his work but says the company's rigid budget won't allow any further merit raises for the time being.

Instead, the boss suggests that the company "won't look too closely at your expense accounts for a while." Should Joe take this as authorization to pad his expense account on grounds that he is simply getting the same money he deserves through a different route, or not take this round-about "raise"?

Survey results: 91 percent of the executives says Joe should turn down the "raise"; 65 percent of the public think he should turn it down. Only 25 percent of the public and 7 percent of the executives think Joe should "take this as authorization to pad his expense account."

The Faked Degree

Bill has done a sound job for over a year. Bill's boss learns that he got the job by claiming to have a college degree, although he actually never graduated. Should his boss dismiss him for submitting a fraudulent résumé, or overlook the false claim since Bill has otherwise proved to be conscientious and honorable, and making an issue of the degree might ruin Bill's career?

Survey results: 50 percent of the executives recommend dismissal; 43 percent recommend overlooking Bill's false claim. 66 percent of the public recommend overlooking the false claim; only 22 percent recommend dismissal.

Sneaking Phone Calls

Helen discovers that a fellow employee regularly makes about $100 a month worth of personal long-distance telephone calls from an office telephone. Should Helen report the employee to the company or disregard the calls on the grounds that many people make personal calls at the office?

Survey results: 76 percent of the executives recommend reporting; 19 percent recommend disregarding the calls. 64 percent of the public recommend reporting, while 26 percent recommend disregarding the calls. When asked what they would say if the amount were only $10 per month, slightly less than 50 percent of those surveyed recommended reporting. But more executives (47 percent) than the public (38 percent) favored disregarding the calls.

Cover-Up Temptation

Bill discovers that the chemical plant he manages is creating slightly more water pollution in a nearby lake than is legally permitted. Revealing the problem will bring considerable unfavorable publicity to the plant, hurt the lakeside town's resort business, and create a scare in the community. Solving the problem will cost the company well over $100,000. It is unlikely that outsiders will discover the problem. The violation poses no danger whatever to people. At most, it will endanger a small number of fish. Should Bill reveal the problem, despite the cost to his company, or consider the problem as little more than a technicality and disregard it?

Survey results: 63 percent of the public and 70 percent of the executives say Bill should reveal the problem and spend the money. Only 25 percent of the public and 24 percent of the executives think Bill should disregard it as a technicality. Reporter Ricklefs adds: "This is the only ethical-dilemma question in which young people are 'significantly more likely to take the stricter ethical option' than their elders, observes Andrew Kohut, president of the Gallup Organization. 'There are great environmental concerns among the young,' he adds."

Discussion Questions

1. Analyze the kinds of moral reasoning you used in thinking through the dilemmas presented above.
2. To what extent, if any, do you think your reasoning was affected by the survey results? What does this suggest to you about your moral reasoning?
3. What do you think surveys like the *Wall Street Journal*'s tell us about ethics?

Last Wish

Is it reasonable to believe that all hospital patients want to be revived if their hearts stop beating? Many doctors think so. And some believe that they have the responsibility to decide for their patients whether they should be resuscitated. However, some recent studies suggest that matters are more complex. Drs. Susanna E. Bedell and Thomas L. Delbanco reported in the *New England Journal of Medicine* that one-third of the 24 mentally competent survivors of coronary arrest at Boston's Beth Israel Hospital in 1981 indicated later that they had not wanted resuscitation and that they would not want it again. But only 1 of the 16 doctors who took care of them suspected that this was how they felt.

In the total survey, only 19 percent of the patients who had been resus-citated had been asked beforehand if they would want it. But 68 percent of the doctors believed they knew what their patients' preferences were. Some doctors indicated that they thought their patients would have brought up the subject if they were opposed to being resuscitated. Others felt they could rely on their patients' nonverbal cues. Some feared that discussing the question with a patient might be so threatening that it could cause a coronary arrest.

In another study, Dr. Arnold Wagner of Evanston, Illinois, interviewed 163 women at a home for the elderly. He reported that 77 said they would not want resuscitation, 64 would leave the decision in the hands of their doctors, 11 indicated they would want it, 10 were incompetent to decide, and one did not return the survey.[18]

Identify and discuss the ethical issues these surveys raise. What are the major values that need to be considered?

The Placebo II

You are a doctor with a patient who has not been feeling very well for some time. He is alternately tense and fatigued. This has affected his sleeping habits. Some nights he lies awake, tense and nervous. The next day he finds himself drooping on the job—even snoozing during breaks. He frequently has headaches and an upset stomach. He has had a physical examination by one doctor already. She had not been able to find anything wrong with him. You have just examined your patient, and you have not been able to find anything wrong with him either. You strongly suspect that your patient's ailment can be resolved by the use of a placebo. Do you think you would be morally justified in deceiving your patient in this way? Explain.

Compare your answer to this question with your answer to "The Placebo I" at the end of Chapter 1.

Law School Admissions II

One of your students is applying to law school. You know that he will be admitted only if you write a strong letter of recommendation. This is because his LSAT scores are only marginally acceptable to law schools. In cases like this, additional evidence of a student's ability to do well in law school is necessary. You honestly believe that he can do well—if only he is accepted. Still, you know that he has not been an outstanding student in your classes. Even though he received A's and B's from you, so did many others. You notice that the recommendation form requires you to rank the candidate in comparison with other students you have had: top 5 percent; top 10 percent; top 25 percent; top 50 percent; bottom 50 percent. Your honest estimate of your student is that he is somewhere in the top 25 percent, but clearly below the top 10 percent. But you are convinced that if he is not ranked in at least the top 10 percent, he might well not be accepted into law school. If he is ranked in the top 5 percent, you think his chances will be very good. If he is ranked in the top 10 percent, his chances will be less good, but you think he might be accepted.

The problem is that, for several years, law schools have received inflated letters of recommendation. The percentile ranking system was introduced by law schools to combat this inflationary trend, but it has continued. Law schools know that the number of students recommended as being in the top 5 or 10 percent is greatly exaggerated. So you fear that if you rank your student as being only in the top 25 percent, law schools will "translate" this to the top 50 percent, at best. How truthful do you think your ranking and letter should be? Explain.

Compare your answer to this question with your answer to "Law School Admissions I" at the end of Chapter 1. Is your reasoning consistent in the two cases?

The Price of a Degree

Cassington College is seriously in debt. It is a high-quality small college, which, like many other small colleges, has had difficulty keeping up with inflation. It needs to increase its funding substantially in order to avoid massive layoffs of faculty—or even a complete closing of the college. But it will lose students if it raises tuition and cuts back on scholarships. As a private college, it cannot receive support from the state. The college has tried very hard to raise funds from alumni and other private sources. But not enough has been raised to solve the problem.

President William Winston is then offered an unusual opportunity. He is approached by a wealthy alumnus, Mr. A. Fluent, who is anxious to make a generous, anonymous gift to the college. But there is a catch. Mr. Fluent's son, Edward, has flunked out of two colleges already. Edward tries hard, but his ability to do college work is questionable. Cassington College's academic standards are quite high, which is why Edward did not apply there earlier. When Edward's application to Cassington was turned down, Mr. Fluent decided to intervene, making the following offer to President Winston: "I would like Edward to be admitted to Cassington and receive his degree within four years. I'll donate $1,000,000 right away if you admit him. As long as he makes satisfactory progress, I'll donate an additional $1,000,000 at the end of each year. When he receives his degree, I'll throw in another $2,000,000. So all you have to do for $7,000,000 is to make sure Edward gets through."

When Winston discusses the proposal confidentially with his good friend and director of admissions, Derek Yerby, Yerby advises: "Go for it. You have to be utilitarian about these things. Seven million dollars will pay a lot of salaries and provide a lot of scholarships for bright and deserving students. So we let one not so bright one through. That's a small price to pay to save a lot of jobs and raise the academic level of the institution. Besides, look at all the big-time athletic programs. They bend the rules to get some of the athletes through. But it helps the school—so they do it."

Next, Winston turns to you, president of the faculty senate. He tells you that what he is about to say is strictly confidential—you should not even share it with your executive board. But he wants your advice. He tells you what Yerby has advised. What do you tell him?

Discuss the ethical issues involved in this situation.

THE PRINCIPLE OF VERACITY

All of us are familiar with lies. Yet providing a satisfactory definition of a lie is not easy. When young children hear something they believe to be false, they often say, "That's a lie!" But a lie is not simply a false utterance. This is so for two reasons.

First, if someone says that 14×55 is 760, this will ordinarily be taken to be a mistaken calculation rather than a lie. To determine whether a lie is being told, it is usually necessary to determine whether the speaker knows, or at least believes, that what he or she is saying is false.

Second, occasionally lies are true statements. A liar might mistakenly believe that what he or she says is false. For example, suppose Karen believes her coworker, Tom, has stayed away from work in order to play golf. To protect Tom, Karen tells her supervisor that Tom is visiting his sick mother. Although Tom had intended to play golf, his mother became ill and Tom, unknown to Karen, has gone to visit her. Nevertheless, it seems clear that Karen has lied.

Typically, but not always, the liar intends the recipient of the lie to believe it. However, in some instances the liar may know that the recipient will not be convinced. The liar might instead be trying to make the recipient think that the *liar* believes the lie. For example, suppose that John wants his poker opponents to think that he is an inexperienced player. He says, "My understanding is that we deal out 8 cards. Is that right?"

To accommodate such cases, we might say that the liar makes an assertion intending to cause the recipient either to believe what the liar has said *or* to acquire a false belief about the liar.[1] But even this definition will not always work. For example, Ruth might wish to convince her friends that she is not as "morally upright" as they accuse her of being. So she tells them a lie that she knows they will recognize as such.

Perhaps we can say that most lies involve *some* intent to deceive.[2] Even Ruth seems to be trying to deceive her friends. In order to convince them that she is not as "morally upright" as they think, she may have to lead them to believe that she is not telling the lie solely for that reason.

Finally, it seems possible to lie without using words at all. One can lie with a shrug of the shoulders or by saying nothing when silence is rightly construed as an affirmation or denial.

Of course, not all forms of deception are lies. Leaving one's radio on when away from home is a deceptive ploy intended to lead thieves to believe that one's home is occupied. But this ploy is not a lie.

Any adequate definition of a lie, should one be found, is bound to be complex and cumbersome. For our purposes, carrying the analysis further is not necessary. We are interested in discussing the fundamental moral questions about lies. A rough characterization that captures most lies will suffice. We will concentrate on standard types of lies, namely, assertions (verbal or otherwise) that are believed by the liar to be false and that are intended to deceive others. Similar moral questions very likely can be asked about those few lies that do not fit our characterization. The same may be true of other types of deception, as well as some nondeceptive types of communication.

The Utilitarian View

To say that someone has lied is, on the face of it, to say something negative about what has been said. This is in striking contrast to our attitudes about the vast majority of activities human beings engage in. To say that someone has been observed walking, talking, playing, working, or eating, for example, does not carry this negative connotation. Lying, like harming, causing suffering, and depriving someone of freedom, seems to call for some kind of justification. In the absence of such a justification, we are strongly inclined to view lying as objectionable.

What is it that makes lying objectionable? A consequentialist answer directs our attention to the consequences of lies, rather than the inherent qualities of lies themselves. For example, Jeremy Bentham, the 19th-century utilitarian, contends: "Falsehood, take it by itself, consider it as not being accompanied by other material circumstances nor productive of any material affects, can never, upon the principles of utility, constitute an offense at all."[3]

But Bentham's most famous utilitarian disciple, John Stuart Mill, was convinced that the undesirable consequences of lying are considerable. While admitting that lying is often expedient in order to avoid embarrassment or to gain an advantage, Mill argues that, on balance, there is more to be said against lying. Mill emphasizes the utility of a particular sensitivity regarding truthfulness. He claims that "the trustworthiness of human assertion" is essential to social well-being and human happiness. He strikingly concludes that "even any unintentional deviation from truth does that much toward weakening the trustworthiness of human assertion."[4]

Sissela Bok, although not a thoroughgoing utilitarian, also has strong consequentialist objections to lying. She claims that liars tend to underestimate the harm and overestimate the good caused by their lies. Those who are caught lying lose credibility and trust. To avoid detection, more lies may have to be told. As more lies are told, resistance to lying breaks down and, with that, one's integrity as well. Victims of lies are often misled into making unfortunate choices. When they discover that they have been lied to, they feel betrayed and lose trust in the liar. Third parties are often misled by lies unwittingly passed on by those to whom lies are told. Finally, lies that seem insignificant can cumulatively result in the undermining of valued institutions and practices (such as in the case of letters of recommendation to law schools).

Bok concludes from these observations that we should accept what she calls *the principle of veracity*. This principle, while not condemning all lies, holds that a negative weight should be attached to every lie. At the very outset, the liar bears a burden of proof that his or her lie is necessary as a last resort. Acceptable alternatives to lying that accomplish the same end are to be sought and, if discovered, chosen.[5]

While sympathetic to the principle of veracity, Margaret Carter is not convinced that an exclusively consequentialist analysis of lying warrants it.[6] Although she concedes that the consequences of lying can be quite harmful, she believes that Mill's estimate is an exaggeration. As a utilitarian, Mill acknowledges that at least some lies are justifiable. But Carter asks, why should we expect *justified* lies to undermine moral character or seriously threaten social trust? Furthermore, although the discovery of someone's lie might throw into doubt the trustworthiness of that individual, this distrust is unlikely to cause us to distrust others. Even to hold, as Bok seems to, that most lies increase the *risk* of various harms does not show that every lie has something to be said against it. A risk of harm is not the same as an actual harm. And if only *most* lies increase the risk, some do not. So why should the principle of veracity be applied to *all* lies?

The utilitarian reply is threefold. First, a justified lie might not threaten to undermine one's moral character, but only if one has first accepted (and met) the burden of proof imposed by the principle of veracity. Second, although a risk of harm is not the same as an actual harm, some risks do result in harms. So if risks are avoidable, they should not be taken. And this is what the principle of veracity counsels. Third, even if some lies do not cause harms, to assume in advance that any particular lie will not is unwarranted. Thus the principle of veracity places the burden of proof on the liar. Reflection might reveal that no harm is likely to result (or that no more acceptable alternative is available). But, Mill and Bok might argue, no lies carry on their face obvious marks that make imposing a burden of proof unnecessary.

So the utilitarian defense of the principle of veracity does not depend on the assumption that every lie has at least some objectionable consequences. Instead, by alerting us to a wide range of undesirable consequences typically associated with lies, it insists that one should not simply *assume* that any particular lie is harmless. From this utilitarian point of view, lies are presumed guilty until proven innocent, rather than innocent until proven guilty. Although some lies might prove to be "innocent," the burden of proof must be met.

Kant's Categorical Imperative

However, many do believe that every lie does have some morally objectionable feature or features. While acknowledging that some lies have desirable consequences, they direct our attention to certain *inherent* features of lies, presenting *nonconsequentialist* reasons for finding lies objectionable. The most extreme example is a view attributed to Immanuel Kant, who apparently believed that one should not lie even to keep a would-be murderer from finding his potential victim.[7] Hardly anyone would agree with such an absolute prohibition of lying. Yet Kant's reasoning should not be hastily dismissed. His fundamental principle, the categorical imperative, bears important similarities to the principle of universalizability. In its first formulation, the categorical imperative says: "Act only on those maxims that you could at the same time will to be a universal law." The liar must ask what he would be approving if he willed lying to be a universal law.

Kant also has a second formulation of the categorical imperative: "Act so that you treat humanity, whether in your own person or in another, always as an end and never merely as a means." Kant regards this to be equivalent to the first formulation of the categorical imperative. This opinion has puzzled many readers of Kant, because the two formulations seem to be saying very different things. However, they are at least connected. For Kant, being capable of acting on the categorical imperative is a mark not only of our rationality but of our dignity. The second formulation says, essentially, that in universalizing our maxims we must be sure to respect the dignity of everyone the categorical imperative applies to. To have dignity is to have intrinsic, or inherent, worth. Money, for example, has only instrumental worth. It is valued not in itself but as a means to something else. Human beings, however, should not be treated merely as a means to an end; they are to be respected as ends in themselves. Human beings are said to be "beyond price."

The idea of human dignity is notoriously difficult to explain. Yet all of us seem to have some sense of what Kant has in mind. This understanding is expressed in statements such as "You're just using me," and in the resentment we feel at being treated manipulatively or at not being treated in ways that respect our right and ability to make rational decisions.

Universal lying, Kant argues, would be self-defeating. Soon, no one would believe what anyone said, and communication would break down. The liar can succeed in deceiving others only if he or she is believed. So the liar can be successful only if lying is not universalized. Because the liar is justified only if universal lying is justifiable, no one should ever lie.

Kant's view seems to imply that if any lie is justified, all lies are justified. But most of us think that not all lies are on the same moral footing. Why, we ask, should we have to agree that justifying one lie justifies all lies? Aren't some lies relevantly different from other lies? Isn't lying in order to take unfair advantage of someone relevantly different from lying in order to prevent a murder?

If the categorical imperative requires us to treat all lies the same, it is unlikely that many will find it acceptable as a moral principle. However, it is not at all clear that the categorical imperative has these implications, even if Kant thought otherwise. If morally relevant differences exist among lies, then these differences should be included in the description of acts to be universalized. Suppose we ask whether we could will it to be a universal law that one should lie *in order to prevent a murder*. Occasions for such lies would be rare; circumstances like this seem strikingly different from circumstances in which one is, for example, simply seeking personal gain or trying to avoid embarrassment. Lies intended to prevent murders would not be self-defeating, as they would not result in a general breakdown in communication. Nor would they lead to any other obviously undesirable consequences.

On the other hand, willing that lying for just any reason whatever, or for no reason at all, be a universal law would have morally disastrous consequences, among them a general breakdown in communication. So, the more moderate Kantian would conclude, one must have a very good reason for lying if it is to be justified. Anything that counts as a good reason in a given situation also counts as a good reason in any relevantly similar situation. While this universalization requirement does not render all lies unjustifiable, it places a severe burden of proof on those who are tempted to lie.

To see how Kantian reasoning might show a lie to be unjustified, consider an example of a lie to gain an advantage. Alex and Roger are the two final candidates for the job of running a new division in the company. One of the responsibilities of the new division leader will be to select company employees for transfer into the division. Fred, along with many others, would very much like to work in the new division. He knows that Alex looks on him much more favorably than Roger does. So Fred considers starting a false rumor about Roger that he hopes will reach the ears of those selecting the new division leader.

Fred now asks whether he could will it to be a universal law that people start false rumors for personal gain. As a first consideration, he might ask how he would feel if the roles were reversed. If he thinks through the situation, he will realize that he would have to find it acceptable for others to start false rumors about him. He would probably resent such treatment. Such resentment would be an expression of his sense of dignity and his moral opposition. Unless he could show that his circumstance is somehow unique in a morally relevant way, consistent reasoning would require Fred to oppose his own lie as well.

It is important to distinguish Fred's reasoning here from merely self-interested, or egoistic, reasoning. An egoist asks what in any particular situation will best promote his or her self-interest. If Fred took this approach, he would first ask how likely his starting a false rumor is to result in bad consequences for him. If he is caught lying, things will probably backfire. Or if his lying is likely to cause others to lie in ways that ultimately will harm his interests, this will count against his lying. That is, from an egoistic perspective, one must consider the likely short- and long-run consequences of the lie.

While not ignoring possible consequences, the Kantian considers them differently. If Fred employs Kantian reasoning, he will not ask how likely it is that he will be caught. Nor will he estimate the likelihood of someday being victimized by a similar lie. Rather, he must apply the principle of reversibility and ask: *If* someone were to lie about me in the way I am contemplating lying about Roger, would I morally object? For the Kantian, to go further and ask how likely such a reversal would be is irrelevant. Enough has been done to demonstrate the wrongness of the lie.

So even if Fred considers only whether he could accept the reversibility of his lie, his reasoning is quite distinct from merely self-interested reasoning; and his lie will not meet the requirements of the categorical imperative. But, from a Kantian point of view, Fred should also ask whether he could condone the widespread practice of lying in such circumstances: "What if everyone were to do that?" This goes beyond the question of whether Fred could accept a reversal of roles. It asks him to consider the consequences of widespread lying of the sort he is contemplating. Opportunities to lie for personal advantage certainly extend well beyond Fred's particular workplace situation. Generalized to relevantly similar situations, Fred's contemplated lie does seem to threaten a general breakdown in communication.

Once again, Fred's Kantian reasoning should be distinguished from a concern about the likely consequences of his lie. Fred is asking what would happen *if* everyone in similar circumstances were to tell such lies. Unlike the utilitarian, he is not estimating the probability that lying will lead to such consequences, or the probability that not lying will prevent such consequences. Instead, Fred might say, "It's a matter of principle, not of actual consequences."

Kant thought his categorical imperative should be used to determine the rightness or wrongness of any action. Although we believe the categorical imperative has considerable merit, we do not accept it as a fundamental grounding for all moral considerations. Some things, such as cruelty, are so obviously objectionable that using the categorical imperative in order to see that they are wrong seems unnecessary. Willing cruel treatment to be a universal law is certainly much more horrible than willing only a single instance of cruelty. But if one could not see what is objectionable in a single instance of cruelty, it might well be wondered if one could see anything objectionable in its universalization.

However, sometimes universalizing does help us see what is wrong with an action. An act might seem relatively innocuous when considered alone, but objectionable when universalized. Consider the smog in Los Angeles during the early 1970s.[8] Presumably everyone in Los Angeles agreed that it was undesirable. A regulation was passed requiring motor vehicles to attach an antismog device. But this device made vehicles less fuel efficient, and gas prices were rapidly rising at the time. Still, let us assume that the widespread use of antismog devices would bring the problem under control.

Now, imagine Jane saying to herself: "As long as enough people keep their antismog devices attached, everything will be under control. If I detach mine, it won't make much difference. I'll save money, and I'll put it to good use. No one will be hurt, and at least one person—me—will be better off!" If Jane is to be successful here, she should not publicize what she is contemplating. If too many people detach their antismog devices, the smog problem will remain. But, Jane adds, "If lots of people detach, I'd be a fool to keep my device attached. My device wouldn't do enough to bring the problem under control. So, either way, I should detach."

Clearly, Jane is reasoning from what she takes to be her self-interest. But she also believes, and plausibly so, that her action, considered alone, will not make matters materially worse. It might even make matters somewhat better overall (especially if she shares her gains with others). However, a Kantian will reject this reasoning. If Jane were to will her action to be a universal law, she would have to approve of all drivers secretly detaching their antismog devices. But she would not approve, because the collective consequences would be undesirable.

The Kantian objection to what Jane is contemplating doing is *not* that it is likely to lead to others doing the same (for it might not); it is that Jane would disapprove *if* everyone were to act as she wants to. For a Kantian, the basic question is one of *fairness*. Jane's success depends on others doing their share. She is taking advantage of their cooperativeness and making an exception of herself.

An interesting question is whether a Kantian would continue to keep the antismog device connected even if most others detached theirs. As a matter of principle, he or she might: "I don't expect my behavior to solve the smog problem. But I think we should be willing to do what is necessary. I'm opposed to going along with something that will harm us now, as well as future generations. Maybe I can't stop it alone. But it's a matter of principle with me."

A utilitarian might go along with this decision—but only if convinced that "acting on principle" sets an example for others that could make a difference. Unlike the Kantian, a utilitarian always asks what consequences are likely. This does not mean that someone with Kantian sympathies will never be concerned with actual consequences. If the consequences of acting on principle would be clearly undesirable, a Kantian might give in. But Jane's compliance would not seem to have such consequences. Furthermore, even if a Kantian acts in order to avoid undesirable consequences, he or she is not, after all is said and done, a utilitarian. Utilitarianism advocates promoting the greatest good for the greatest number. The only concession the Kantian is making here is that one should be concerned to avoid bad consequences (whether for the greatest, or a more limited, number). Maximizing good consequences implies limiting bad consequences. But the reverse implication does not hold.

A Breach of Faith

Utilitarians do not claim that all lies are inherently objectionable. We have argued that, sensibly understood, Kant's categorical imperative cannot condemn all lies as a matter of moral principle. While agreeing with this argument, Margaret Carter offers a Kantian view that even justifiable lies have an inherently objectionable feature: Every lie is a *breach of faith*. According to Carter, making an assertion indicates to others that one is expressing one's mind, creating a right on the part of the listener to expect, or assume, that the speaker has expressed his or her mind.[9] A lie conflicts with this right.

Similarly, Charles Fried holds that asserting a statement is "inviting belief by reference to or in the context of the institution of asserting—or more abstractly, the institution of communication."[10] He continues, "it is simply that institutions by which people, when they make statements to each other, invite belief, and not belief based *on the evidence* of the statement so much as belief *on the faith* of the statement."[11] Making an assertion is like making a promise. One gives one's assurance that the statement is true. It is this giving of assurance that makes a lie a breach of faith.

According to Carter, this breach of faith is the wrong-making feature that attaches to every lie. Even though consequences might add to the wrongness of a particular lie, Carter concludes that *every* lie is morally wrong unless counterbalancing reasons exist. Thus she supports Bok's principle of veracity, but on nonconsequentialist grounds.

Of course, the principle of veracity only places a burden of justification on the liar. It does not by itself settle questions of justification. Shortly, we will explore in some detail how these questions should be approached. First, however, we will present one more defense of the principle of veracity—this time from a consideration of character.

Lying and Character

So far we have considered defenses of the principle of veracity that focus on *conduct*. But some attention should also be given to considerations of *character*.

Joseph Kupfer has recently presented a defense of the principle of veracity that examines relationships between lying and character.[12] His view can be outlined in terms of the following claims.

All lies have two *inherent* negative features: (1) Lying imposes an immediate (but not necessarily long-run) restriction of the deceived's freedom. (2) Every lie involves *self-opposition*, an internal conflict that results from speaking what one disbelieves.

Each of these features has a connection with another harm: (1a) Restricting another's freedom by lying inclines the liar in the direction of *disrespect for others*. (2a) Self-opposition in lying threatens the *integration* of the liar's personality. These harms are tendencies, not necessary consequences. For example, lack of sleep may incline one toward irritability and making mistakes. This does not mean that those deprived of sleep are *always* irritable or error-prone, but that they are likely to be.

These four claims, for Kupfer, warrant a presumption against lying. Although this presumption can be overridden by other considerations, Kupfer's point is that it must be if lying is to be justified. Furthermore, these four claims direct our attention to how the liar is affected by lying as much as to harms suffered by the deceived. What is at stake is the character or personality of the liar.

First consider (1) and (1a), the restriction of freedom and the tendency to disrespect others. A successful lie interferes with the deceived's practical exercise of reason. By providing the deceived with misinformation, the liar is seriously affecting how the deceived will perceive his or her options. This is a restriction of freedom, at least in the short run.

Often the liar's freedom is increased in relation to the deceived, thus placing the liar at a relative advantage. Since lying initiates this advantage, it disposes the liar toward a general habit of disrespect. Again, Kupfer points out, this is a matter of likelihood, not inevitability. Still, if a habit of disrespect for others develops, it is a character defect or vice, one often associated with a form of arrogance, or inflated self-esteem.

Kupfer claims that this disrespect is to the *humanity* not only of the deceived but of people generally. It is only against a background of general truthfulness on the part of others that the liar can succeed. Quoting Charles Fried, Kupfer says that lying attacks the deceived "with an *instrument* (language) *that belongs to him*: the indignity of being struck with one's own property."[13]

Next, consider self-opposition and the tendency toward personality disintegration. Kupfer says that the content of a lie is "antagonistic to what the individual is."[14] The liar's beliefs and actions don't match up. Kupfer makes two psychological points: First, he says that a natural, and healthy, transition takes place between belief, thought, and speech. Lying has a tendency to undermine this continuity of self. Second, we have no "inherent motive force" to make someone else believe what we do not ourselves believe. Kupfer concludes:

An inherent end of speech is the communication of belief. . . .
[L]ying runs counter to this natural end of language. Kant puts it
this way: The liar "has a purpose directly opposed to the natural
purposiveness of the power of communicating one's thoughts." Since
the liar necessarily *shares* in this "natural purposiveness" of language,
he opposes himself by lying.[15]

In order to sustain a lie, the liar has to prevent others from discovering
the lie. The ways the liar can interact with others become limited. According
to Kupfer, not only is the liar's freedom restricted, so is his or her self-
knowledge, because we depend to some extent on truthful interaction with
others in organizing our opinions and coming to know ourselves.

Both self-knowledge and personality integration are important for the
moral life. Self-knowledge, says Kupfer, is "inescapably part of the moral
[person], if only because so many moral virtues depend upon it."[16] Personality integration is a necessary condition for moral goodness, and even for
being able to resolve moral perplexities: "Without some level of personality
coherence, it makes no sense to speak of someone either beset by moral
difficulties or in a state of moral anguish."[17]

Kupfer identifies several vices associated with lying: cowardice, lack
of self-restraint, and self-indulgence—all forms of moral weakness. No
doubt we regard these as moral weaknesses in part because they are associated with harms to others, but Kupfer presents a strong case for concluding
that lying poses a risk of serious harm to the liar as well—namely, to his or
her character.

While not condemning all lies as unjustifiable, the principle of veracity does insist that liars bear the burden of justification. We have looked
at a variety of reasons in support of this principle. Even if no one kind of
reason applies to all lies, it is still possible that the combination of reasons
supports the principle of veracity. Sometimes we may be more concerned
about a breach of faith than any immediate or long-range consequences of
a lie. At other times we might be more concerned about possible harms—
to others, to valued practices, or to the liar's character. In any case, in the
next chapter we will consider what justifying lies requires. We will not
approach questions of justification from either an exclusively consequentialist or an exclusively nonconsequentialist perspective. Both approaches
seem to us to have something to be said for them. But we are not convinced
that any one moral principle or theory is adequate to organize all of our
moral concerns. In many instances, diverse moral principles will support
the same conclusions about what should or should not be done—but for
different reasons. It does not seem to us that moral principles can be
arranged in a hierarchy in the abstract. Sometimes a Kantian concern for

fairness may supercede considerations of the general good. At other times, however, it may seem justifiable to allow utilitarian considerations to override fairness to some. More important for our purposes is to outline procedures that it would be reasonable to follow as we attempt to think through situations that call for moral reflection.

Withholding Information

On August 7, 1985, the Associated Press reported White House spokesman Larry Speakes's defense of his withholding information about a cancerous growth on President Reagan's nose. (The growth was a basal-cell carcinoma, the most common and easily controlled form of cancer.) Defending his credibility, Speakes said: "Did I lie? No. Did I tell the truth? Yes. Did I mislead? No." A reporter claimed that Speakes had "pulled an iron curtain down on the truth." Speakes replied, "Exactly right, but I did not lie and I told the truth."

Speakes had not revealed that a spot had been removed from the president's nose until he was questioned several days after the surgery. (Some reporters had noticed a scar on the president's nose.) He had no comment when asked whether he thought more information should have been given to the press earlier. When asked how similar situations might be treated in the future, Speakes replied, "I'm sure . . . it would be handled differently. Sure." He did not elaborate.

Speakes said that refusing to reveal information "does not constitute a lie." He refused to tell the press when he first learned that a biopsy was being performed on the growth. He commented, "I don't customarily discuss what I knew and when I knew it."

When the president said he learned a biopsy was being performed conflicted with when Speakes knew it would be—Speakes apparently knew before the president. When asked how that happened, Speakes replied, "See if you can figure that out."

Discussion Questions

1. Do you think that Speakes's withholding of information was deceptive or misleading?

2. To what extent does the public have a right to know details about the health of its president?

3. Does your answer to #2 imply that a president has less right to withhold information about health matters from the public than private citizens do? If so, why?

A Different Bird

Author James Herriot relates the story of Mrs. Tompkins and her budgie, Peter.[18] Herriot, a veterinarian, visited the home of the frail and elderly widow to clip the beak of her budgie. Peter had not been his usual self lately, and Herriot thought clipping his beak might revitalize him. As Herriot reached into the cage and gently picked up the budgie, it fell limp in his hand. Peter, apparently frightened, had died from heart failure.

Near panic, Herriot decided he should not tell Mrs. Tompkins that her pet had died. The loss, he felt, might be too devastating to her. He realized that she had not noticed what had happened—she had poor eyesight and was hard of hearing. So he quickly rushed Peter out of the house, explaining that he would be better able to do the job in his office.

Herriot found a suitable substitute budgie at a bird store. Placing "Peter the Second" in the cage, Herriot assured Mrs. Tompkins that all should now be well.

For some time Herriot avoided visiting Mrs. Tompkins. Finally he decided he should stop by. Worried that she might have discovered that Peter the Second was an impostor, Herriot reluctantly entered Mrs. Tompkins's home. She greeted him by saying, "You know, you wouldn't believe it, he's a different bird." Harriot swallowed hard, "Is that so? In what way?" "Well," replied Mrs. Tompkins, "he's so active now. Lively as can be. You know he chatters to me all day long. It's wonderful what cutting a beak can do."

Herriot told what might be called a *benevolent* lie. Is this an example of a justifiable lie? Were there any other acceptable alternatives for Herriot? Discuss.

A Coach's Credibility

In February 1985 the Detroit Lions announced that Darryl Rogers would become the new coach of the professional football team. A barrage of criticism from the Detroit newspapers immediately followed. Sportswriters had not forgotten the circumstances of Rogers's resignation as head coach at Michigan State University in 1980 in order to become head coach at Arizona State University. To these writers, history seemed to be repeating itself. We have excerpted three of the critical responses below.

Rogers Packs Big Problem: Credibility

Profile of a gypsy:

"I am the football coach at Michigan State. I plan to stay at Michigan State. I have had no offers to leave." Jan. 15, 1980, East Lansing.

"I am in a bind. If the folks at Arizona State had handled this correctly, we wouldn't have any problem." Jan. 16, 1980, East Lansing.

"It's a pleasure to be here at Michi . . . Arizona State University. . . .

The thing I left the Midwest for was the opportunity to come back to the West." Jan. 18, 1980, Tempe.

"I have a feeling for contracts. I never left one before." Jan. 18, 1980, Tempe.

"I have no [had, *sic.*] discussion with anyone in Detroit. No, I am not a candidate." Feb. 5, 1985, Phoenix.

"We have just had a 35-minute meeting and he says he has not signed a contract with Detroit. He has assured us that the rumors are false and that he is Arizona State's football coach." Feb. 6, 1985, 12:30 p.m., Tempe.

"The Detroit Lions announce the appointment of Darryl Rogers as their head coach and director of football operations." Feb. 6, 1985, 12:50 p.m., Pontiac.

"Oh, I just called Detroit after I got out of the meeting and we finalized everything." Feb. 6, 1985, 1 p.m., Tempe.

Darryl Rogers begins his career as head coach and reigning wizard of the Lions under the black, ugly cloud.

Darryl has the pizzazz, all the razzmatazz that William Clay Ford has long desired in his football coach.

Rogers also had a splendid gift for words. It is unfortunate that the words are not always the truth.

Darryl Rogers will be in Detroit for as long as the mood strikes him—and Bill Ford.

But henceforth no one will ever know what is to be believed or not believed.

That's an extremely serious problem. The Lions in their haste to discover their next head coach created a graver problem for themselves.

That new problem is credibility.

Monte Clark, with all his faults,

was a man whose every statement could be accepted as gospel.

Of course, if those Roman candles go shooting off over the sidelines and the points spin around the scoreboard, it won't matter an awful lot what he tells people. The fans ache for a winner.

This whole atmosphere, sadly again, reflects the mood of society today. Trust doesn't matter very much at all—except to the naive.

Winning is the only ethic that counts. . . .

Rogers . . . wanted to hold the hiring announcement until next week. He wanted to complete his recruiting mission for Arizona State. The deadline for national letters of intent is next Wednesday.

That way, Arizona State wouldn't suffer so much the loss of its football coach at the height of the recruiting drive. The recruits would be in.

But then the young men who were recruited into Arizona State would be accepting offers with the belief that Darryl Rogers was going to be their head coach.

What does it matter that a few college kids had got themselves duped?

What hurts as much as anything is that there isn't a more sincere, trustworthy, candid man in town than William Clay Ford.

But now Darryl Rogers is coming to town. Maybe he'll get Bill Ford to buy a used car from him.[19]

Rogers: All I Want Is a Chance with Lions

TEMPE, ARIZ.—It probably was a harmless remark, spoken with a smile and a silly chuckle after a 45-minute interview in a nearly vacant television studio. But after so many recent instances of deception, of needless denial and contradiction, it has become difficult to determine whether Darryl Rogers says anything with full practical intent.

"You know that I haven't signed my contract with Detroit yet," he said.

No, you tell yourself, he can't be serious. He's joshing. Surely he would not break his verbal agreement with the Lions and return to Arizona State.

Or would he?

No one really knows anymore, not after the confusing and bizarre developments that have taken Rogers from the sun, the mountains and the impending pressure of a pivotal 1985 football season in Tempe to a rebuilding situation in Detroit that doesn't demand immediate success. . . .

Most significant of the doubts, Darryl Rogers is being questioned about his credibility, his integrity, and his honesty. He has explained the scenario of his hiring in too many different ways. He told his athletic director one story, the Phoenix media another, the Detroit media yet another. Nothing matches. For instance, when an *Arizona Republic* reporter asked Rogers where he had spent Tuesday afternoon, Rogers claimed to have met with a recruit in Chicago. But the prospect, Chuck McCree, told the newspaper that he never met with Rogers Tuesday. . . .

"Nobody likes to be looked at poorly, but most of the things people say about you aren't controllable. So you let things be," he said. "I'm going to Detroit to win football games. If we win, the atmosphere will be fine. If not, then let them come at me."

"All I want is a chance."[20]

Such fibs might not have mattered had this been someone other than the same Mr. Rogers who, with three years left on his Michigan State contract, denied through his teeth that he was talking to anyone from Arizona State. Next day, he was going, going, gone. It was one thing to be sworn to secrecy about a new job, in an attempt to plug leaks, but it was quite another to look the truth squarely in the eye and instantly begin to squint.[21]

Discussion Questions

1. List and discuss important moral and ethical observations made by the sportswriters in the above columns. Can you think of any others?

2. Do you agree that all will be forgiven and forgotten if coaches (or athletes) like Darryl Rogers are "winners"? Should it be?

CHAPTER SIX

JUSTIFICATORY PROCEDURES

It is tempting for those considering whether or not to lie to confine themselves to questions of practical strategy. Thus, the inquirer might reflect: "I am faced with a practical problem. What strategy is likely to be the most successful in dealing with this problem?" There is no assurance that posing the problem in this way will focus on the moral dimensions of lying. One's objective could be to escape an embarrassment or inconvenience. It could be to benefit oneself, a friend, or a loved one. Such objectives are not inherently objectionable. However, lying to accomplish them should raise moral questions.

Our discussion of the principle of veracity explains why many think that liars bear a special burden of proof. The principle of veracity is a moral principle, not just a principle of practical strategy. Those who take this principle seriously can be said to have internalized it in such a way that they feel some moral resistance to lying even when tempted to lie. To the extent that one has internalized the principle of veracity, he or she has the virtue of truthfulness. This virtue involves having an initial disposition not to lie. However, dispositions are only tendencies and offer no guarantee that one will not sometimes fall short of the ideal. Furthermore, the principle of veracity does not require one always to be truthful. It maintains only that the liar bears a burden of proof and that one should lie only as a last resort, after other more acceptable alternatives have been sought.

Understood in this way, the principle of veracity is quite demanding. This stringency can be supported by pointing out the many ways in which lying can conflict with what matters to us. Lies can harm those who tell lies, those to whom lies are told, third parties affected by the lies, and social and political institutions we value. Even the so-called harmless lie can exact a cumulative toll when it is an instance of a widespread practice which is harmful. Furthermore, reasonable alternatives to lying are available to us much more frequently than we tend to realize. This suggests that we tend not to be reflective enough about the circumstances in which lies are told.

More adequate reflection about lying requires us to pay close attention to differences between the perspectives of deceivers and those who are deceived. Those who lie frequently fail to appreciate how those to whom they lie might feel about being deceived. This is so even when the lies are intended for the supposed good of the deceived, especially when the lies are paternalistic. At the same time, those who are deceived frequently fail to understand fully the perspectives of those who deceive them. But if we are concerned with moral justification, all relevant perspectives must be understood and taken into consideration. In addition, the consequences of lies for third parties, for relationships between people, and for valued social and political institutions and practices must be considered.

In attempting to take into account all relevant considerations, it is important to realize that there is no decision procedure available to us that eliminates the need to exercise judgment in particular cases. We can identify a variety of types of reasons that might be offered in support of or against lying in various circumstances. But these reasons might be weighted differently in different circumstances, and there are times when they might conflict with each other.

Although general considerations of harm, benefit, and fairness, for example, are relevant criteria to bear in mind in attempting to justify a lie, it is not clear how they might be arranged hierarchically in the abstract. In some cases avoidance of harm seems to be more important than considerations of fairness; in others, the reverse may be the case. Rather than advocate some one principle from which judgments about the justification of lying might be derived, we advocate a pluralistic position that remains sensitive to the subtle differences among various contexts.

Levels of Justification

As an alternative to providing *answers* to our perplexities about lying, Sissela Bok suggests a set of procedures for attempting to resolve our perplexities about lying.[1] We will now describe and comment on those procedures.

Conscience

Bok's first level of justification is the appeal to one's conscience. Suppose that someone who accepts the principle of veracity is nevertheless contemplating telling a lie. Such a person has a predisposition against lying. Unless convinced that no other morally acceptable alternative is available, he or she will not lie without a troubled conscience. Couldn't such a person simply consult his or her conscience, especially if this incorporates a concern for universalizability, whether in the form of the golden rule, Kant's categorical imperative, or some notion of generalizability? Bok's reply is that even though an appeal to conscience may be necessary, it often is not sufficient. This is because even those with the best of moral intentions are prone to rationalization and narrow vision (egocentricity). Vested interest in certain outcomes and unnoticed bias can block the fuller vision required by moral justification. Also, an appeal to conscience might not just be too permissive. It could also be too restrictive. So, with the aid of others, one might come to see that a lie that is initially regarded unconscionable is actually justifiable.

Peer Consultation

As a second level of justification, Bok suggests we consult with peers—or at least try to imagine what our peers might think. But this consultation might not be sufficient. Just as an individual can be egocentric, a group of individuals can be like-minded and, therefore, limited in understanding and biased in its outlook. This phenomenon has been effectively documented by Irving Janis in his *Victims of Groupthink* (which we will discuss in detail in Chapter 7). "Groupthink" supports the "right-mindedness" of members of the group while ignoring or suppressing opposing views. Thus critical thinking is restricted.

The Test of Publicity

So Bok suggests a third level of justification. Here the audience is widened to include a representative sampling of possibly divergent points of view. At this level, one must try to convince an audience of representative, reasonable people that one is justified in lying. Bok calls this step the *test of publicity*.

Ensuring that the audience is a truly representative and reasonable sample is difficult. Nevertheless, we believe that the ideal of consulting a group of representative, reasonable people provides a useful model for moral justification. Unfortunately, Bok says relatively little about what such people might be like. So we will make some suggestions.

A reasonable person is someone who is open to reasoning with others, not just on his or her terms but from a sharable perspective. A person can fall short of being reasonable in many ways. He or she may exhibit one of the forms of unreasonableness: for example, selfishness; excessive partiality toward particular people, groups, or organizations; a willful resistance to considering the full range of relevant factors. Or individuals might lack reasonableness about certain matters because they lack the relevant experience, knowledge, or imagination. Although not necessarily unreasonable, such individuals cannot be said to be reasonable about matters that require the experience, knowledge, or imagination they lack.

We are interested in the idea of reasonableness insofar as it can be linked to the idea of moral justification. If what we do never had any effect on the well-being or interests of others, moral justification would be of little, if any, interest to us. To attempt to justify a point of view is to offer reasons in support of it that, ideally, can be found acceptable to anyone capable of rationally considering it, not just to oneself. This is not an easy task. Those who take it seriously can be said to be attempting to be reasonable (that is, to reason with others).

The possibility of moral justification rests on the availability of a basis for agreement among those willing to take questions of justification seriously. What do human beings have in common that might provide such a basis for agreement? Vulnerability is one shared trait. We are all susceptible to pain, suffering, sorrow, unhappiness, frustration, impairment, disability, and death. Second, we are all capable of achieving some satisfaction of our interests and, as a result, some degree of self-fulfillment, pleasure, and happiness. Third, all of us are to some extent dependent on others in getting what we need and want. Aside from the usefulness of cooperative endeavors and some division of labor, our well-being also depends on the restraint of others from harming us. Fourth, we may share expectations, goals, and hopes with others. Fifth, all of us, to at least some extent, value caring relationships with others. Sixth, self-respect and self-esteem are important to each of us; neither flourishes without the support of others.

Finally, we are capable of fair-mindedness, respect for others, compassion, and benevolence. Those who are deficient in these features seem willfully to resist approaching matters in a reasonable manner. Those who lack fair-mindedness show an unwillingness to view matters impartially, focusing on special interests (either their own or those of limited groups). Those who have no respect for others show a disregard for their rights. Those lacking in compassion or benevolence display an indifference to, if not hostility toward, those whose interests should be taken into consideration.

But fair-mindedness, compassion, and benevolence in an individual might not be enough. One might lack relevant experience, knowledge, or imagination. For this reason Bok is right in insisting that the test of publicity depends on the reflections of *representative*, reasonable persons. In many instances, it is unrealistic to think that any one individual has sufficient background and imagination to perceive all morally relevant perspectives.

This limitation is recognized by ethics review committees in hospitals, as well as institutions that do research on human beings or animals. An attempt is made to select individuals to serve on these committees who are not only reasonable but sufficiently representative that, as a group, they can be expected to take into account all relevant perspectives.

Thus ethics committees should have considerable diversity, drawing from various professions, as well as individuals not otherwise affiliated with the institution whose activities are being reviewed. This gives greater assurance of representativeness, but not in the sense of individuals lobbying in behalf of the "constituency" they "represent." This would be to politicize the procedure. In practice, some politicization may be inevitable. However, the selection of *reasonable*, representative individuals minimizes this. A mark of a reasonable person is his or her willingness to attempt to address issues from a point of view that could be acceptable to others. Thus a reasonable person, recognizing his or her limitations in background or imagination, should actually *welcome* the assistance of others in trying to learn and take into consideration all relevant factors.

Reasonableness should not be equated with rationality. Someone can be unreasonable but still rational. For example, someone who is extremely egoistic, or self-interested, might exhibit a high degree of rationality in the pursuit of self-interest. It is only when rationality is combined with fair-mindedness, respect for others, compassion, or benevolence that we can expect one to exhibit much in the way of reasonableness.

Frank Sibley nicely sums up what we are trying to say about reasonableness:[2]

> If I desire that my conduct shall be deemed *reasonable* by someone taking the standpoint of moral judgment, I must exhibit something more than mere rationality or intelligence. To be reasonable here is to see the matter—as we commonly put it—from the other person's point of view, to discover how each will be affected by the possible

alternative actions; and, moreover, not merely to "see" this (for any merely prudent person would do as much) but also to be prepared to be disinterestedly *influenced*, in reaching a decision, by the estimate of these possible results. I must justify my conduct in terms of some principle capable of being appealed to by all parties concerned, some principle from which we can reason in common.

Impartiality

Bok's test of publicity, with its reliance on the notion of representative, reasonable people, is aimed at achieving a kind of *impartiality* in moral reasoning. However, some care must be taken in explaining what this impartiality requires. Impartiality comes into play at two levels in morality. First, impartiality is required in morally justifying kinds of actions, practices, rules, or principles. The principle of universalizability holds that what is right or wrong for one person is right or wrong for any relevantly similar person in relevantly similar circumstances. It insists on impartiality in determining what kinds of actions, practices, rules, or principles are morally acceptable. Identification of particular, actual people or groups is to be excluded. This prevents particular persons or groups from making unfair exceptions of themselves.

However, this requirement of impartiality should not be confused with impartiality at a second level. It is quite likely that some practices or rules can be impartially approved even though they themselves allow for partiality in the treatment of individuals. Family members and friends show partiality to one another. The father who insists on paying as much attention to all children as to his own would be employing an unusual sense of impartiality. He probably would not give enough love and care to his own children. At the same time, the kinds of partiality toward others we find desirable should be consistent with practices or rules that can be justified impartially.

In some cases, partiality toward loved ones is morally objectionable. For example, if a teacher's daughter is a member of his class, partiality toward her should be discouraged. If the teacher is either lenient or severe with his daughter, a moral complaint is in order: He will either be unfair to the other students or to his daughter.

The requirement to be impartial in our specific relationships does not automatically follow from the idea that the justification of certain actions, practices, rules, or principles requires impartial reasoning. The kind of impartial reasoning required by justification should have us ask: Can we impartially support an action, practice, rule, or principle that permits (or even requires) some persons to be given preferential treatment because of the special relationships they have to someone? The answer is: sometimes, yes—subject to certain limitations.

Seeing that impartiality can be understood at these two different levels sheds some light on the controversy between Carol Gilligan and Lawrence Kohlberg introduced in Chapter 4. At his highest level of moral reasoning, Kohlberg seems to require impartiality in both senses we have discussed. Moral principles must be impartially chosen. But these principles seem to require, for Kohlberg, impartiality at a more specific level as well. Thus Kohlberg maintains that Heinz should be as prepared to steal a lifesaving drug for a stranger as for his wife. Justice and respect for the right to life are the highest values. Gilligan, however, urges us to consider a morality of care—one that shows greater sensitivity to particular relationships and the particular contexts of moral decisions. Gilligan, too, would insist that the principle of universalizability be satisfied, but she does not see this as implying that universal principles of justice and rights as necessarily taking priority over love, friendship, and caring. Heinz's love for his wife can be as good a reason for stealing the drug as his respect for human life—it may even be a preferable reason.

Whatever Heinz is said to be justified in doing must be universalizable to others in similar circumstances. But this is consistent with arguing that stealing to save the life of a loved one is relevantly different from stealing to save the life of a stranger. Whether stealing to save either life is justified depends on the situation. But even if one concludes that someone in Heinz's situation has a duty to steal for his wife, it would not follow that he has a duty to do the same for a stranger. Gilligan would insist that we, again, look carefully at the context, including the special relationships that exist. In principle, it seems that there are many potentially universalizable positions for which one might argue. For example: It is morally allowable for Heinz to steal for his wife, but not for a stranger; or it is morally allowable for him to steal for either; or it is morally required that he steal for his wife, but it is only allowable that he do so for a stranger; or it is not allowable for him to steal for either, but it is somewhat excusable for him to steal for his wife; and so on.

Original Position

Contemporary philosopher John Rawls provides a useful model for the kind of impartiality required by moral justification.[3] He presents a hypothetical situation in which self-interested individuals are placed in what he calls an *original position*. A "veil of ignorance" is imposed on them. They are temporarily deprived of special knowledge about themselves that often biases their judgments in their own favor. For example, they do not know their race, whether they are male or female, wealthy or poor, well educated or poorly educated, healthy or sick. The knowledge they have is restricted to general facts about human psychology, economics, governments, and the like. Under these circumstances, Rawls asks, what fundamental principles of justice would these individuals propose to use in evaluating the basic social and political institutions of their society?

In answering this question, unanimity is required to ensure that all individuals will be heard and that the majority cannot simply ignore minority views. Once the veil of ignorance is lifted, individuals would be expected to remain committed to these principles. The veil of ignorance forces the individuals to imagine what it would be like to end up in each social-political position in society once the veil is lifted—for any position might, for all they know, be theirs. In effect, the veil of ignorance serves to coerce otherwise self-interested individuals to think impartially.

Rawls uses original position only in regard to fundamental principles of justice. However, we might attempt to use it to ask what guidelines individuals in the original position would recommend concerning lying, maintaining confidentiality in professional-client relationships, and so on. This would require each of us to work much harder than we usually do at trying to imagine what it would be like to be in the positions of all who have some stake in what kinds of communication take place.

Of course, any attempt to satisfy the requirements of Rawls's hypothetical original position or Bok's appeal to representative, reasonable people may fall short of the ideal of the test of publicity. Nevertheless, as an aspiration, Bok's third level of justification has much to commend it. Bok makes no claim that this aspiration is always realizable. She simply urges one to conscientiously attempt to pass judgments through the requirements imposed by the test of publicity. Here we are reminded of John Stuart Mill's insistence that "[i]n order to find the truth we must hear all arguments in their most persuasive form."[4] Mill, like Bok, emphasizes the importance of hearing all arguments, from a variety of perspectives, including that of the minority. For Mill, 99 percent of the task of adequately supporting one's point of view is being able to defend it against opposing views.

Guidelines

What guidelines for evaluating lying might come into play at Bok's third level of justification? Although we agree with her that the test of publicity works only imperfectly, we share her concern to combat our egocentric tendencies with appeals to a more impartial perspective. This perspective takes into account the deceived, deceivers, and third parties, as well as our concern for social and political institutions and practices.

Bok identifies four kinds of reasons commonly cited in attempting to justify a lie:

1. To avoid harm.
2. To produce benefits.
3. To promote or preserve fairness.
4. To protect a larger truth.

The first three can be divided further. Harms can be more or less severe, short term or long term, and so on. The harm to be avoided might be to the liar, to the person to whom the lie is being told, or to third parties. Of course, the lie might avoid harm to the liar but cause harm to someone else. Even the reverse is possible. Similar observations need to be made about lying to produce benefits or to promote or preserve fairness. Furthermore, the kinds of harms or benefits can be made more specific. For example, a harm could be painful suffering, lost opportunities, or a deprivation of autonomy.

Other complications are possible. The avoidance of one kind of harm may be at the cost of another. A lie told to protect the deceived from suffering might also prevent the deceived from making a decision. For example, a paternalistic lie, although intended for the benefit of the deceived, also interferes with his or her autonomy.

We would add to Bok's list four more kinds of reasons commonly given for lying:

5. To comply with an expectation or order by one's supervisor or employer.
6. To be loyal to another.
7. To maintain confidentiality.
8. To respect the wish of others not to be told the truth.

It might be argued that each of these kinds of reasons is subsumable under the four identified by Bok. Failure to meet the expectations of one's employer, for example, can result in harm to oneself (demotion or loss of job) or perhaps to others. But respect for authority and "doing one's job" seem, for many at least, to be reasons in their own right. (Whether they are good reasons, however, needs to be considered carefully.) Similarly, acting from loyalty or from a commitment one has made to preserve confidentiality seem distinguishable from (1)–(4) and common enough to warrant special attention.

Number 8, lying in order to respect the wish of others not to be told the truth, poses special difficulties. Of course, not telling someone the truth does not always require lying. Remaining silent may be an alternative. Also, not wanting to be told the truth is not the same as wanting to be lied to. If Oscar does not want to be told that he has a terminal illness, for example, it does not follow that he wants his doctor to lie to him. What he wants is to be healthy. Fearing that he might be terminally ill, Oscar might simply try to avoid his doctor. Or he might behave in such a way that his doctor senses that Oscar does not want to hear the truth. Nevertheless, Oscar still might not want to be lied to. Were he to learn that his doctor had lied to him about his condition, Oscar might react with anger even though the news would have been unwelcome.

However, if Oscar did want his doctor to lie to him about his terminal illness, his doctor might, nevertheless, have good reason not to lie to him. It is possible that Oscar would be better off knowing the truth even if he doesn't want to hear it. That possibility aside, even if Oscar would never discover the lie, or not resent it once he discovered it, others might realize that a lie was told. This realization might reduce their trust in the word of the doctor, creating fear and distrust in that doctor and, perhaps, doctors in general.

Similar remarks could be made about intimates or associates not wanting to hear the truth about their qualities or abilities. For example, a lover might not want to be told that he is not handsome, debonair, or romantic, and he might be pleased to be told that he is handsome, debonair, or romantic. But this does not imply that he wants to be lied to about these matters. Teachers might not want to hear that they are not good teachers, but they also might not want to be lied to about their teaching.

However, the fact that people do not always want to hear the truth does complicate matters for those who possess it. Our point is not that this is *never* a sufficient reason for lying. But we are saying that, even taking into account the fact that one does not want to hear the truth, a lie is not necessarily warranted.

Still, what these examples point out is that those who are lied to or deceived are not necessarily passive receivers of the lies they are told. Sensing that one's listener does not want to hear the truth certainly can be a *psychological* factor that partially explains why some lies occur. Even if this factor does not justify the liar, it indicates that the deceived may bear some responsibility for being lied to.

The Placebo III

You are on the medical staff of a hospital. You have been appointed to a committee whose task is to develop a set of guidelines for the acceptable use of placebos by your medical staff. Your committee is concerned about the possible bad effects of the indiscriminate use of placebos. A local citizens' committee has recently drawn the public's attention to unethical uses of placebos in the treatment of patients. The hospital committee includes a member of the local citizens' committee. This person is not on the medical staff of the hospital.

1. What guidelines will you recommend to your committee? Explain the rationale behind them.

2. If your recommended policy holds that the use of placebos is sometimes justifiable, describe a concrete situation in which it would be. Describe a situation in which it would not be. Explain the differences between the two cases.

3. Apply your recommended policy to "The Placebo II" at the end of Chapter 4.

Law School Admissions III

Consider the situation in "Law School Admissions I" in Chapter 1 from the following perspectives:

- The director of admissions of Western State's School of Law, who receives the letter of recommendation for the student.
- Students applying to Western State who really do belong in the top 5 or 10 percent.
- Other students applying to Western State who belong in the top 25 percent and whose letters of recommendation place them at that rank.

We have presented several versions of the law school admissions case. The first time we tried out these different versions, we divided our class into three groups, representing the perspectives of the student, the professor, and the law school admissions official. The results were quite interesting. All but one member of the group representing the student thought that the professor should inflate the student ranking. Those responding to the professor's version had mixed answers. Roughly half thought the professor should inflate the ranking somewhat, while the other half thought the professor should be as truthful as possible. Those responding to the admission officer's version were unanimous: The professor should be as honest as possible. As might be expected, when the groups discussed their answers with one another, the need for more careful inquiry into questions about honesty and deception became apparent.

We have also asked students to write out answers to the different versions. Below are some of the responses we have received. Compare these responses with your own.

Admissions Officer

"Law schools are not playgrounds, nor lawyers recreationists. It is the intent of law schools to produce knowledgeable attorneys with a solid academic and social base to serve a greater societal good. A truthful recommendation can be the first step in setting this in motion. One must look above and beyond individual and personal ambitions to a higher ideal; the greatest good for the greatest number."

"I realize that letters of recommendation are meant to *recommend,* but I feel that dishonest letters may injure the futures of students who actually do possess outstanding characteristics. Let's say as an administrator I decided to ignore all the letters that were loaded with praise, deeming them exaggerations. This action hurts those students who have worked hard as undergraduates and deserve the praise they have received in their letters of recommendation."

Professor

"Professional responsibility must be separated from personal feelings."

"In a sea of lies, a student who is competing with better, equal, and lesser students will drown."

Student

"If the law school already expects the ranking to be inflated, then it would be useless to send in an honest ranking."

"He is not really lying, because the system has already lied."

"I would presume a truthful response. But if the professor has a practice of exaggerating, I would expect a higher recommendation."

A Question of Candor

When Children's Hospital in Buffalo, N.Y., hired a new anesthesiologist last summer, officials were confident that Dr. Arif Hussain was just the sort of doctor they were looking for. A graduate of the University of Bologna School of Medicine, the Pakista-

ni-born physician had trained at Boston's prestigious Brigham and Women's Hospital. Furthermore, he was preceded by four glowing letters of recommendation from his senior colleagues. The Buffalo doctors were shocked when police officers showed up with a warrant for Hussain's arrest: He was charged with sexually assaulting two women patients in Waltham, Mass. And then, to their utter astonishment, it turned out that two months before being hired by Children's Hospital, Hussain had been found guilty of rape. (*Newsweek*, Oct. 5, 1981.)

According to the *New York Times* (Sept. 24, 1981), one of the letters of recommendation was dated the day after Hussain's conviction (with two other doctors) for raping a nurse after taking her from a late-night party in Boston to a Rockport beach house owned by one of the doctors.

Hussain had pleaded not guilty, and he was free pending appeal of his conviction. He and the other doctors had been sentenced to three to five years, with the sentences suspended to six months. Under Massachusetts state law, a doctor who commits a felony can automatically have his or her licence revoked. No action had been taken against Hussain, however.

The trial had been given headline coverage in the Boston papers. But apparently news of the trial had not reached Buffalo. In any case, none of the letters of recommendation mentioned Hussain's legal difficulties. Doctors at Brigham and Women's Hospital said that the Buffalo hospital never questioned them about Hussain's application. However, Thomas Sullivan, spokesman for Children's Hospital, said that Buffalo doctors had phoned Brigham and Women's to verify the letters of recommendation. He commented: "We did not receive candid and complete information."

One of the letters of recommendation described Hussain as "one of the most knowledgeable and skilled residents in anesthesiology I have ever worked with." The other letters were equally supportive. One of the letter writers commented that the crime Hussain was convicted of was "absolutely not relevant" to his professional ability.

Various doctors offered their opinions about letters of recommendation. Here is a sampling of views reported in *Newsweek* and the *New York Times*:

"Letters of recommendation are worthless. I have been given advice by our hospital lawyer, if you want to make a derogatory remark to do it by phone, and to do it from a pay phone." Otherwise, commented this doctor, you might have a $250,000 lawsuit against the hospital. "You have to weigh whether telling the truth is worth that much money."

On letters for less than outstanding colleagues, one doctor commented: "I usually praise the strong points and gloss over the weak ones, but a discerning employer will pick these weaknesses up."

Another doctor said that all doctors were now aware that letters of recommendation have become cheapened. He suggested that the Buffalo hospital should have made follow-up phone calls.

On the other side, however, was Dr. Stanley Wyman, president of the Massachusetts Medical Society: "This was an indiscretion, a failure of true candor." Wyman said that he would bring this case before the society's ethics committee for investigation.

Other doctors agreed with Wyman. Dr. Burton J. Lee of New York's Memorial Sloan-Kettering Cancer Center said of the letter writers: "They'll be seriously damaged in the medical community." Dr. Brad Cohn, a San Francisco pediatrician, commented, "If the person you recommend doesn't measure up, your future credibility is zero."

B. J. Anderson, associate general counsel for the American Medical Association, said that the AMA advises directors of departments in hospitals to be candid in letter writing, despite the threat of lawsuits. However, he added, "too frequently hospitals that have had a problem with a doctor will write a glowing letter because it is easier to export your problems across a state line than to resolve them yourself."

Discussion Questions

1. Imagine that you are a member of the Massachusetts Medical Society's ethics committee. Dr. Wyman has presented the above information to your committee. Assume for the sake of discussion that, in fact, the Buffalo hospital did make follow-up phone calls. What do you think the ethical issues are? Discuss.

2. Did the doctors who wrote the letters of recommendation for Hussain *lie*, or were they simply not candid? Is the distinction between lying and not being candid morally important in situations like this?

3. Does the mode of communication (by letter, over the telephone) make a difference in regard to what is morally appropriate to say about a job candidate? Discuss.

4. Have students play various roles in the Hussain case representing the perspectives of those who might be concerned about what did or did not take place. Possible roles: Buffalo hospital administrators; doctors writing for Hussain; Hussain; prospective patients (and their parents) of the Buffalo hospital; the head administrator at Brigham and Women's Hospital; the nurse who claims to have been raped; the patients who claim to have been sexually molested by Hussain; the medical profession; society as a whole; those who lost out in the competition for the Buffalo job given to Hussain.

Guidelines for Persuasion

In attempting to determine what principles of justice we should use in evaluating the fundamental structure of our social and political institutions, John Rawls suggests that we imagine ourselves placed in a hypothetical situation he calls the "original position." The original position deprives us of the special information about ourselves that often biases our outlook when making moral judgments. We are to imagine ourselves deprived of knowledge of our sex, race, educational level, wealth, and the like.

Use the original position to try to determine guidelines for morally appropriate and inappropriate kinds of persuasion. Imagine how these guidelines might be applied in a variety of communication settings: advertising, persuasion in a salesroom, promotion of sales over the telephone, solicitation of contributions for a worthy cause, a lecture or discussion in a college classroom, a public address, advice in a professional-client relationship.

APPLICATIONS AND CASES

THE PROBLEM OF "GROUPTHINK"

Our discussion of moral reasoning has so far concentrated on individual decision making. However, most of us also work with others in groups or organizational settings. Individual decision making has a place there, too. But many jobs involve *group* decision making—in executive committees, review committees, task forces, divisions or departments. And some families and social groups make group decisions. In these settings, *interdependence*, rather than independence (or dependence), is primary. The autonomy of the solitary decision maker takes a back seat to the give-and-take of group interaction and joint endeavor.

Although group decision making is significantly different from individual decision making, it, too, is subject to moral appraisal. Group decisions can be responsible or irresponsible, just or unjust, fair or discriminatory, respectful of or in violation of rights, sensitive or insensitive to the needs and interests of others, and so on. In contrast to individual decision making, however, the locus of responsibility is difficult to pinpoint. Although individuals play an essential role in group decision making, just what that role is (or ought to be) is less than clear. As we will see, how individuals understand their roles and how their roles are understood by others in the group have an important bearing on the moral qualities of group decision making.

In any complex social or organizational setting that is not totally autocratic, some group decision making is necessary. It is also desirable. Although our society extols the virtues of individual accomplishment and competitiveness, cooperation is also seen as necessary to accomplish common ends and to fulfill our needs of sociability. As important as individual independence is, we are highly interdependent both physically and socially.

In addition, we live in a society that values participatory democracy. Thomas Nilsen has argued that respect for the individual involves respect for one's capacity to make "significant choice." In group decision making, "significant choice" could be acknowledged in voting. However, not all group decision making involves voting. Perhaps we should say that individuals should be allowed "significant voice."

Allowing individuals "significant voice" in group decision making does more than acknowledge their right to meaningful participation. It also can increase the likelihood that groups will make morally acceptable decisions. This outcome is suggested by Bok's test of publicity. Although she proposes it as an aid to individual decision making, a literal application of the test would require group deliberation. Representative points of view are presented, listened to carefully, and evaluated from a sharable perspective.

But group dynamics can pose serious obstacles to a more objective outlook, even though group deliberation can often serve as a corrective to individual bias and shortsightedness. We will now discuss some of these obstacles.

Social psychologist Irving Janis has made a careful study of groups that are characterized by high cohesiveness, solidarity, and loyalty.[1] These are qualities that are quite desirable to most of us. But Janis has found that many cohesive groups become victims of their own "groupthink": a tendency for groups to arrive at agreement at the expense of objective, critical thinking.

Janis arrived at his conclusions about groupthink after studying various historical fiascos. He discovered that groupthink contributed to bad decision making by those who were responsible for U.S. security at Pearl Harbor before our involvement in World War II. According to Janis, the group responsible ignored warning signs that the Japanese would attack. An entire U.S. fleet and thousands of lives were lost when the Japanese bombed Pearl Harbor. Janis cites several other misfortunes that involved groupthink: our government's failure to realize that Communist China would retaliate after U.S. troops crossed the 38th parallel during the Korean War; the Kennedy administration's miscalculations concerning the invasion of the Cuban Bay of Pigs; and the Nixon administration's underestimation of the public outcry the Watergate affair would provoke.

Although Janis focuses on major fiascos in his book, he emphasizes that groupthink occurs in groups of all kinds—committees, boards, teams, work units, and so on. In the film *Group Dynamics: Groupthink*, a fictitious corporate meeting is used to illustrate groupthink phenomena. Janis then discusses this example in some detail.[2] Since this setting is more typical of the kinds of situations most of us are likely to encounter, we will concentrate our discussion on the film's example. We hope that readers will have an opportunity to view the film as well.

Marketing Byrotonin: A Case Study

The film opens with Phil, the marketing manager, being approached by Dr. Heller, a staff scientist who is a member of the research team that has been testing Byrotonin, a weight-reducing drug. Heller is concerned about the results of the tests, which suggest that taking Byrotonin can have harmful effects on some people. Phil denies his request to discuss this problem at the board meeting about to convene. Heller insists that he needs only a few minutes of the board's time. But Phil replies: "We've got to polish this thing off. I know what's in the report. So I'll take the information with me. All right? We've got to polish it up. We've got to get the product on the market. So do us a favor, will you—the big man's going to be there. We've got to wrap it up today. We just don't have any choice."

The scene shifts to the boardroom. The company president opens the meeting: "We have only one item to discuss today, and I think we can wrap that up rather briefly—whether or not we proceed with the marketing of Byrotonin, our new weight-reducing pill.

"We've all known each other a long time, long enough to see this company grow into one of the major factors in our industry. One of the reasons I'm excited about Byrotonin is that it can allow us to continue this growth. It should also allow us to increase our dividends to our shareholders. They've been behind us, and they deserve the kind of reward that Byrotonin can bring.

"I also know that some outside test reports have come in that are not completely positive, and I want these brought up today."

Then Phil presents an optimistic report on the expected profits over the first few years, concluding, "Simply put, this means we can make a lot of money with a very good product—and at the same time we can make a lot of unhappy fat people a little thinner and a little happier." [Laughter and smiles from the group members.]

The president asks one of the company lawyers whether the necessary legal clearances have been received. He responds: "We're okay in D.C. Of course, the FDA may reexamine after a year on the market. [Pause.] The only problem is those outside tests. [Pause.] If more unfavorable results come in—well, those FDA guys love to be troublemakers."

"Sure," adds the company's public relations executive, "it gets them good press. The government's protecting the poor taxpayer!"

The president calls on Jerry, the research manager: "Jerry, as the house pessimist, how do you read those reports?"

"Obviously my department wouldn't have recommended Byrotonin unless we felt it was basically safe," Jerry replies. "But still, some of those reports that came back from our sample group of doctors aren't too good—" Jerry is interrupted by the president, who quickly asks, "What percentage, Jerry? What percentage of the reports are negative?"

"Oh, very small, less than 2 percent."

Jerry is then asked about the seriousness of the symptoms. He replies: "Well, one doctor reported vomiting with one of his patients. Another suspected blood clots. One patient had dizzy spells."

"That's not very dramatic stuff," one member retorts.

Another adds, "They sound like the kinds of symptoms that could be brought on by anything. That kind of data is not very conclusive. Besides, we pick our physician sampling at random. Some of those doctors could be quacks or professional cranks. Now, we know we've got the best people in our labs. They are the ones we ought to trust."

The president turns to another company lawyer, Harriet, and asks whether she sees any liability problems. She responds somewhat hesitantly, "Oh, you know a lawyer doesn't like to be pinned down in advance. The problem is that precedents for this kind of a situation aren't that clear-cut. The safe answer would be to test further."

"If lawyers had their way," Phil interjects, "the whole industry would still be just making aspirin!"

Another group member says, "It's a strict prescription-only product. Any doctor who doesn't feel sure about it doesn't have to prescribe it."

"Not only that," concludes the public relations executive, "we have built one of the finest reputations in the field by dealing squarely with the public. We're not about to endanger that with a faulty product."

The president intervenes: "Okay . . . all right. Let's try to stay together on this. I'm sure Harriet wasn't trying to upset the apple cart." He asks Phil about the memo from Heller, the research scientist who was not allowed into the meeting. "Did you talk to him about it?"

"That's why I was late," says Phil. "He caught me as I was coming in. His sentiments, as always, are basically conservative. It was the usual stuff about wanting to test more and so on. But knowing how rushed we were, I thought I'd relay this information. Otherwise we'd just be sitting here for 30 minutes listening to him."

The research manager is asked about Heller's negative recommendation and adds that Heller is a minority of one. "The rest of the research group is quite confident and has been very conscientious."

The public relations executive urges, "Let's go with it. We don't have anything to worry about."

"Anyone else?" asks the president. [Brief pause.] "I guess it's unanimous. We go with it."

Janis asserts that groupthink especially occurs in highly cohesive groups in which members have strong, positive feelings toward the group and a desire to remain in good standing in the group. Strong feelings of solidarity ("we-feeling") pervade such groups.

One of the consequences of high cohesiveness, says Janis, is a tendency of members of the group to strive toward agreement. This concurrence-seeking tendency is at the heart of groupthink. Janis explains that in the Byrotonin example, the group failed to explore clear indications that the drug might have problems:

> They didn't consider the possibility that they might be letting themselves in for some real trouble. This has happened in a number of instances in which drugs were marketed before they were adequately tested and has led to very serious consequences. So this is an example of how the failure to engage in critical thinking, as a result of this striving for concurrence, can lead to potential trouble. This doesn't always occur, but that potentiality is certainly there.[3]

Janis has identified eight major symptoms of groupthink, all of which are present in the Byrotonin case.

1. He notes that an *illusion of invulnerability* runs through the entire discussion in the board meeting. It underlies the group's willingness to take excessive risks.

2. The strong "we-feeling" of a cohesive group can result in a tendency to look at outside groups as adversaries or enemies. This is often expressed in shared *stereotypes*. In the Byrotonin example, shared stereotypes were manifested in statements such as "Those FDA guys love to be troublemakers" and "Some of those doctors could be quacks or professional cranks."

3. *Rationalization* occurred a number of times, Janis continues. The group came up with statements that attempted to shift responsibility to others: "It's a strict prescription-only product. Any doctor who doesn't feel sure about it doesn't have to prescribe it."

4. The moral tone of rationalization contributes to the *illusion of morality*. Statements are made that proclaim the inherent morality of the group, enabling the group to avoid serious discussion of the moral implications of their decisions. By saying, for example, "We have built one of the finest reputations in the field by dealing squarely with the public," the group can go on to do what it wants to do, comfortable with the thought that the company has always "done the right thing."

5. But why is it that no one in the group feels free enough to stand up and say "Wait a minute. We're kidding ourselves. We may be about to make a terrible mistake."? A basic irony in group psychology, says Janis, is that the freer the climate in the group, the greater is the tendency toward *self-censorship*. Because they can speak out if they want to, members censor their own statements.

6. Contributing to this self-censorship is the *illusion of unanimity*. Members do not express their doubts, even if they have them, because they assume that everyone else's silence implies consensus. There is a reluctance to disrupt group unity. When the group is about to make its final decision about whether to market Byrotonin, the president asks, "Anyone else?" Silence is construed as consensus. This moment of silence, Janis observes, encourages self-censorship. Everyone has the sense that others are in basic agreement, and none really want to rock the boat.

7. If a member does begin to express doubts, however, *direct pressure* is applied to encourage conformity. This is evident in an earlier part of the discussion when Harriet suggests that further testing is advisable. When this suggestion is resisted by some members of the group, the president quickly intervenes. But rather than asking Harriet to elaborate, he tries to bring the group back together by saying, "Let's try to stay together on this. I'm sure Harriet wasn't trying to upset the apple cart."

8. Finally, *mindguarding* takes place. Janis says that a mindguard is similar to a bodyguard. Just as a bodyguard protects one from being physically harmed, a mindguard protects one from being exposed to disturbing ideas. Phil, the marketing manager who kept the scientist from attending the meeting, functions as a mindguard at the outset of the film. His move keeps the president and other members of the group from hearing opinions that could be quite divergent from their own. Phil, it should also be noted, further reduces the likelihood of

taking Heller's concerns seriously by stereotyping him: "His sentiments, as always, are basically conservative. Just the usual stuff about
wanting to test more, and so on."

Janis's observations about groupthink are invaluable in enabling us
to see why groups often fail to exhibit the kind of critical thinking that is
essential to responsible decision making. To his list we will add one more
observation. Often individuals in groups find safety in numbers. Since no
single individual is fully responsible for a group decision, it may be easier
to go along with the group. Quite apart from the desire to be accepted by
other group members, an individual may take comfort in the thought that
"we decided," rather than "I decided." If faced with full responsibility for
whatever decision is made, an individual might have decided differently
from the group.

This possible diffusion of individual responsibility within groups adds
to the responsibility of group leaders. In the Byrotonin example, the president actually promotes groupthink. His opening remarks stress group ca-
maraderie and loyalty. They also suggest that the matter to be discussed
can, and should, be handled expeditiously. His primary goal seems to be
to win consensus on moving quickly ahead with the marketing of Byrotonin.
Critical thinking is discouraged.

Janis suggests some ways to promote critical thinking in groups.
Primary responsibility falls on the group leader to provide an atmosphere
conducive to critical thinking. Allowing adequate time for reflection and
discussion is essential. The Byrotonin meeting was rushed. Either earlier
meetings could have been arranged to discuss the testing problems, or the
decision could have been postponed until the group had an opportunity to
more thoroughly consider the issues raised.

A group leader can also emphasize to group members that each has
a basic responsibility to serve as a critic. Some of the other responsibilities
group members should accept include: adequate preparation for discussion,
careful thought, concern for the group's discussion process, objectivity, good
listening skills, and a willingness to share one's reflections with others.
Responsible members who are not willing to support the group's recommendations should make their dissent known *while* the group is deliberating,
perhaps by submitting a "minority report" of some sort. This may not change
anyone's mind, but at least the effort will have been made. In some circumstances, responsible, dissenting members may take the serious step of seeking outside help in blocking a group's actions. This might involve going
over the head of one's immediate superiors within an organization or "blowing the whistle" on the organization itself.

This role need not detract from group cohesiveness, as long as it is understood that serving as a critic is essential to promoting the group's ends. After the Bay of Pigs fiasco, Janis notes, President John F. Kennedy explicitly assigned the role of critic to his Cabinet members. He also called in outside critics. Finally, recognizing that the presence of the group leader might subtly suppress free, critical discussion, Kennedy sometimes deliberately stayed away from some meetings about matters that called for independent, critical advice.

Groupthink: Some Ethical Considerations

Irving Janis's observations about groupthink should alert us to some ethical concerns about group decision making.

It is important, first, to acknowledge the significance of the role of groups in our society. Groups often have a practical advantage over individual effort in meeting the basic societal needs for food, shelter, health care, entertainment, transportation, and the like. An extraordinary amount of time, effort, and money is invested in group deliberations and decision making. As we have already noted, this form of decision making results in many benefits. Individuals often get psychological benefits from working well with others—social acceptance, security, an enhanced sense of self-worth, and so on.

Groups can, in varying degrees, satisfy or frustrate basic social needs. William Schutz claims there are three major needs that can be satisfied in group interaction: the need for inclusion, the need for affection, and the need for control.[4] If some group members feel excluded, unappreciated, or powerless, it may indicate morally flawed group interaction. When significant ideas are glossed over or ignored, as they often are in groupthink situations, people walk away from the meeting feeling unfulfilled and dissatisfied. Their sense of self can be diminished if they hold conflicting ideas but are reluctant to verbalize them in group meetings. A certain self-opposition can result, which may also affect their self-esteem. The reputations of individuals involved in groups that make bad decisions can suffer as well. Their thought processes can be impaired to the extent that they develop habits of uncritically accepting flawed reasoning.

The hindsight of astute researchers such as Janis might suggest that groupthink phenomena are relatively easy to detect. Not so. The Byrotonin example was in many respects exaggerated in order to identify and illustrate the eight symptoms of groupthink. More subtle cues need to be noticed in actual group settings.

Bad decisions by groups can also cause people to lose confidence in group decision-making processes. This loss of confidence is particularly troublesome in a society that values democracy in both the workplace and government affairs. One alternative to group decision making is to have decisions made in autocratic and authoritarian ways.

Free and full discussion is an important right. It enables participants to see the various options available to them, whether as decision makers themselves or as a part of a decision-making body. Groupthink fails to provide room for the exercise of the right to "significant voice."

The lack of free and full discussion presents another, but related, problem. Groupthink favors the quick and unreflective adoption of majority opinions, with minority opinions being discouraged. But minority opinions should be welcomed. As John Stuart Mill insists, "In order to find truth we must hear all arguments in their most persuasive form." Mindguarding, self-censorship, the illusion of unanimity, and direct pressure all discourage the verbalizing of minority opinions. Manipulating who is given an opportunity to speak, intentionally fogging or distorting dissenting views, and railroading ideas are other familiar techniques for squelching minority viewpoints. Mill gives four basic reasons why minority opinions should be given a full hearing:[5]

- The minority view might be right.
- The minority view might not be wholly right, but it might contain an important element of truth.
- Even if the minority opinion is not right, the majority opinion will be understood more fully if it is openly defended against a dissenting opinion.
- If majority opinions are not openly defended against dissenting opinions, they run the considerable risk of becoming "dead dogmas."

A serious problem is the tendency for individuals not to accept responsibility for decisions made in a group, even though they may have participated in the decision making. "After all," one might say, "it wasn't *my* decision; it was the *group's*. Even if I had opposed the group's decision, it wouldn't have changed anything—I'm only one person."

In the public sphere, citizens have a right to know what their leaders are thinking and to have the opportunity to question decision makers. Meetings of public bodies generally should be open and announced in advance, with some indication of the agenda. Although much of the work of a deliberative body is understandably conducted outside the meeting room (by committees, officers, and staff), the decisions and their rationale should be made public.

As we will see in the next chapter, a group may be held morally accountable by the public for using flawed processes of deliberation and decision making. Group leaders have a responsibility to minimize this problem by encouraging effective communication within groups and between levels in organizational structures. But all members of groups bear some responsibility for resisting groupthink and for making sure that morally relevant concerns are given a fair hearing.

Discussion Questions

1. What is groupthink? What symptoms of groupthink are identified by Janis?

2. How does groupthink interfere with critical thinking?

3. Do you agree that there are serious ethical problems associated with groupthink? Discuss.

4. How do group leaders contribute to groupthink? What might they do to prevent it? Do they have an ethical responsibility to do so?

5. How do other group members contribute to groupthink? What might they do to prevent it? Do they have an ethical responsibility to do so?

6. Analyze the Byrotonin case. To what extent was groupthink present? What ethical problems are associated with groupthink in this case?

7. Write a case study from your own experience in which you think groupthink was present. Discuss the symptoms of groupthink that were present, their possibly harmful effects, and the ethical responsibilities of members of the group to prevent groupthink.

ETHICS IN ORGANIZATIONS: THE CHALLENGER EXPLOSION

We have discussed how groupthink can obscure individual responsibility and discourage the kind of critical thinking needed in responsible decision making. However, even if these problems are successfully resolved by individual groups, these groups may report to larger organizations. Just as an individual cannot always act as an autonomous decision maker, a group of individuals may be similarly constrained. A division within a large organization, for example, often only makes recommendations to a higher organizational level. Those recommendations may or may not be made known to those at the highest level, where the ultimate responsibility for decision making lies. This stratification can give rise to further ethical problems. In this chapter we will consider some of these problems, particularly those that involve communication.

Large organizations have complex, hierarchical structures. Various groups of individuals typically work in relative isolation from one another. For example, sales, manufacturing, and research divisions within a large organization all contribute to the goals of the organization, but they may

Written with Ronald C. Kramer, Ph.D., Criminal Justice Program, Department of Sociology, Western Michigan University.

have little direct contact with one another. Furthermore, the various lower divisions of an organization may not have a very clear idea of how their contribution fits into the larger objectives of the organization. Coordination of the efforts of these different divisions is accomplished at higher levels.

Insofar as lower divisions in an organization lack "the big picture," those working at that level may find it difficult to morally assess their situation. Some may find comfort in the notion that their job is simply to fulfill the requirements of their job description or the stated goals of their division—or, perhaps, simply to "do what they're told." Essentially, this attitude attempts to push responsibility to the top.

However, the view from the top may not be as clear as it should be. It cannot be assumed that upper-level management always has ready access to all the information from lower levels that should be considered in responsible decision making. To some extent, this failing may be a consequence of the delegation of responsibility to middle-level management.

How this responsibility is delegated can make a difference. Some executives or upper-level managers might establish that, in some areas at least, their directive is: "Here's what you should accomplish. Do it, but don't tell me how you get it done." This policy can have the effect of obscuring responsibility. As those at lower levels attempt to push responsibility up, those at higher levels attempt to diffuse it. When something goes wrong, those at lower levels might say that they were just doing what they were told. Those at higher levels might reply that they "accept responsibility" for what took place but insist that they were unaware of what was happening at the lower levels.

However, such a cynical view of managerial policy isn't necessary to account for breakdowns in the flow of critical information. More subtle factors often are involved—factors that obscure individual responsibility even more and that suggest that flaws in organizational structures may need as much attention as the moral shortcomings of individuals. A tragic illustration is the *Challenger* explosion. The detailed Rogers Commission report provides ample evidence that even our most respected organizational structures are vulnerable.

A System Breaks Down

On January 28, 1986, the space shuttle *Challenger* exploded in midair, sending six astronauts and schoolteacher Christa McAuliffe to their deaths. The initial public reaction was shock and disbelief. Americans had come to expect routine flights from NASA. Well before the shock had eased, the public wanted to know why the accident took place. Some of the reasons surfaced almost immediately, and they were disturbing.

The press reported that engineers at Morton Thiokol, the contractor responsible for building the solid rocket booster, had vigorously opposed the launching of *Challenger*, but their warning had not been heeded by management. These engineers suspected what the Rogers Commission would later support, that the immediate cause of the explosion was a burn-through of the solid rocket booster joint O-rings—the same O-rings that engineers had been concerned about for more than eight years.[1]

Despite this concern, top NASA decision makers (at levels I and II) told the Rogers Commission that they had no knowledge on January 27 that these matters had been the subject of intense controversy within Thiokol and between Thiokol and the Marshall Space Flight Center (levels IV and III in the decision-making chain). These officials added that they would not have given the final approval to launch if they had heard the views of the Thiokol engineers.

After a careful study of the variables contributing to the *Challenger* explosion, the Rogers Commission concluded that although the O-ring failure was the immediate cause, a flawed decision-making process was an equal, if not more important, contributing factor. The major findings of the commission:

1. The Commission concluded that there was a serious flaw in the decision-making process leading up to the launch of flight 51-L (the Challenger flight). A well structured and managed system emphasizing safety would have flagged the rising doubts about the Solid Rocket Booster joint seal. Had these matters been clearly stated and emphasized in the flight readiness process in terms reflecting the views of most of the Thiokol engineers and at least some of the Marshall engineers, it seems likely that the launch of 51-L might not have occurred when it did.

2. The waiving of launch constraints appears to have been at the expense of flight safety. There was no system which made it imperative that launch constraints and waivers of launch constraints be considered by all levels of management.

3. The Commission is troubled by what appears to be a propensity of management at Marshall to contain potentially serious problems and to attempt to resolve them internally rather than communicate them forward. This tendency is altogether at odds with the need for Marshall to function as part of a system working toward successful flight missions, interfacing and communicating with the other parts of the system that work to the same end.

4. The Commission concluded that the Thiokol management reversed its position and recommended the launch of 51-L, at the urging of Marshall and contrary to the views of its engineers in order to accommodate a major customer.[2]

The first three conclusions focus on internal processes at Thiokol and Marshall. The fourth conclusion, however, directs attention to "a major customer." This reference raises the question of whether concern to serve a customer can result in compromises in areas of quality control and safety. If so, further examination of the fourth conclusion might shed further light on the problems identified in the first three conclusions.

In the *Challenger* case, decisions were made that ultimately resulted in the deaths of seven people. These decisions were made from structural positions within a network of contractually related organizations. We need to consider organizational factors that may have contributed substantially to these decisions. We will concentrate on three salient factors: (1) NASA *goals*; (2) *structural strains* within NASA; and (3) the *adequacy of controls* at NASA.

NASA Goals

The idea of a reusable spacecraft that could provide frequent, economical access to space first surfaced in the late 1960s during the height of the *Apollo* program. In September 1969, a Space Task Force report to the president offered a choice of three long-range plans. In varying combinations, these plans called for (1) a manned Mars expedition; (2) a lunar-orbiting space station; (3) an earth-orbiting station; and (4) a space shuttle to link the orbiting station to earth.[3]

In March 1970, President Nixon made an important political choice. For budgetary reasons, he scrapped the Mars project and the space platform, but he ordered the development of the shuttle vehicle. As the Rogers Commission points out: "Thus the reusable space shuttle, earlier considered only the transport element of a broad, multi-objective space plan, became the focus of NASA's near-term future."[4]

This decision forced NASA to put all its eggs in one basket; it significantly shaped NASA's goals for the future. From this point on, to prove that the shuttle could be used as a universal launch vehicle, NASA tried to create an operational shuttle system by instituting a heavy schedule of flights.

Pressure on NASA to make the space shuttle a universal launch vehicle increased dramatically in the 1980s under the Reagan administration. Including the initial tests, the space shuttle flew 24 successful missions.

There was pressure to declare the space shuttle "operational" and no longer "developmental"; pressure to make the shuttle system an economically self-sufficient commercial cargo hauler; and pressure to develop a major role for the space shuttle in the military space program.

Ronald Reagan took office just as the space shuttle program was preparing to launch its first test flight. In August 1981, the president established an interagency review of U.S. space policy. The group's deliberations, which took place as NASA completed the first four orbital test flights, resulted in the "Presidential Directive on National Space Policy." This directive was issued in conjunction with Reagan's first major speech on space, delivered at Edwards Air Force Base on July 4, 1982, the day the initial orbital tests concluded.

In this speech, Reagan announced a national policy to set the direction of the space program during the following decade. As part of that policy, the president stated, the shuttle system "is the primary space launch system for both national security and civil government missions."[5] Reagan went on to declare the space shuttle fully operational and thus ready for a wide variety of important tasks:

> The fourth landing of the *Columbia* is the historical equivalent to the driving of the gold spike which completed the first transcontinental railroad. It marks our entrance into a new era. The test flights are over, the groundwork has been laid, now we will move forward to capitalize on the tremendous potential offered by the ultimate frontier of space. Beginning with the next flight, the *Columbia* and her sister ships will be fully operational and ready to provide economical and routine access to space for scientific exploration, commercial ventures, and for tasks related to the national security. Simultaneously, we must look aggressively to the future by demonstrating the potential of the shuttle and establishing a more permanent presence in space.[6]

The president's declaration that the space shuttle was "fully operational" exerted enormous pressure on NASA. An operational system is one that has moved out of the research and development phase, where problems and mistakes are expected and looked for. By the time something is operational, the bugs in the system are supposed to have been worked out. Yet was this true of the shuttle system? No, say a number of experts. They argue that the system was still in the research and development phase and that the president had prematurely labeled it operational.[7]

The Reagan administration was eager for the shuttle system to become operational because it had developed some rather ambitious commercial and military goals for NASA. One of these goals was for NASA to become an economically self-sufficient cargo hauler, primarily of communication satellites.[8] Thus NASA found itself in the business of launching satellites for a wide variety of customers.

According to the Rogers Commission, pressures in NASA increased as a result, perhaps at the expense of engineering considerations:

> Pressures developed because of the need to meet customer commitments, which translated into a requirement to launch a certain number of flights per year and to launch them on time. Such considerations may occasionally have obscured engineering concerns. Managers may have forgotten—partly because of past success, partly because of their own well-nurtured image of the program—that the shuttle was still in a research and development phase.[9]

Nevertheless, the decision to include a schoolteacher, Christa McAuliffe, on the *Challenger* flight reaffirmed President Reagan's message to the public that the shuttle system was fully operational. The explosion of the *Challenger,* however, reminded us all that we still could not take space flight for granted.

In addition to the pressure of commercial concerns, NASA was increasingly asked to use the space shuttle for military purposes. From the very beginning, NASA was, for the United States, an important element in the science-technology race related to military interests and objectives.[10] As the shuttle system came to be the centerpiece of the space agency's projects, pressure to militarize its missions, from the Congress, the Pentagon, and the White House, became more frequent.

The president's 1982 directive instructed NASA to "preserve United States preeminence in critical space activities"; keeping the space shuttle on an accelerated flight schedule was described as "vital and critical" to the national defense. The directive went on to say that "launch priority will be provided for national security missions."[11] Pressures on the shuttle program escalated even more the next year with the announcement of Reagan's "Star Wars" plan. Whatever form the Strategic Defense Initiative would eventually take, the testing and development of such a space missile defense system would require an operational space shuttle capable of making a very large number of flights on a regular schedule.

It is evident, then, that NASA was subjected to strong external pressures to accept very ambitious goals. These goals were internalized within the organizational structure of NASA. The agency committed itself to a frenetic pace of launchings in the 1980s, at one point proposing 714 flights between 1978 and 1990.[12]

This pressure was undoubtedly felt by individuals at NASA. It was this launch pressure that led Marshall Space Flight Center solid rocket booster project manager Lawrence Mulloy to comment, on hearing the

Thiokol engineers' objections to the *Challenger* launch, "My God, Thiokol, when do you want me to launch, next April?" Thus external pressures were internalized as organizational goals by NASA, zeroing in on individual decision makers and setting the stage for the *Challenger* explosion.

Structural Strains Within NASA

As NASA attempted to meet the increasing flight schedule of the space shuttle and achieve the commercial and military goals that had been laid out for it, the agency encountered a number of constraints and operating problems. These constraints made it increasingly difficult for NASA to reach its goals in an acceptable way—that is, with the high level of safety expected of it. The disjunction between the organizational goals of NASA and acceptable means available to meet these goals created structural strains within the agency. Apparently NASA attempted to resolve these strains by resorting to means that were less safe, rather than by changing its goals and proceeding more cautiously.

The first source of structural strain directly related to the *Challenger* disaster was the faulty seal design of the joint on the solid rocket motor. The faulty design, of course, was the responsibility of Morton Thiokol, the contractor for the solid rocket motors. The Rogers Commission, however, also assigns fault to NASA, for failing to act on information concerning the flaw:

> The genesis of the *Challenger* accident—the failure of the joint of the right solid rocket motor—began with decisions made in the design of the joint and in the failure by both Thiokol and NASA's solid booster project office to understand and respond to facts obtained during testing. The Commission has concluded that neither Thiokol nor NASA responded adequately to internal warnings about the faulty seal design. Furthermore, Thiokol and NASA did not make a timely attempt to develop and verify a new seal after the initial design was shown to be deficient.[13]

The Rogers Commission found written objections to the design as early as October 1977. In addition, the commission discovered that the O-ring seal had been designated a "Criticality 1" feature of the solid rocket booster design in 1982. "Criticality 1" meant that the O-rings had been identified as a failure point—without backup—that could cause the loss of life or vehicle if the component were to fail.[14] On the day before the launch, a delay because of the weather was debated. The weather was expected to be much colder than any conditions in which the O-rings had been tested.

More than 30 people were in at least 25 communication situations during this period discussing the O-ring problem. Yet none of the concerns reached levels I or II.

If the design was flawed, rendering the O-rings insufficiently safe, it seems reasonable to conclude that they should have been redesigned and made more safe. But to do so would have greatly slowed down the space shuttle's flight schedule, which would have met enormous resistance.

How did NASA resolve this strain? Some NASA officials responded by keeping the space shuttle flying and failing to inform higher-level officials of the severity of the design flaw. The problems with the faulty seal design were defined as "not serious" and as an unavoidable and acceptable "flight risk." Even so, enough concern had been raised that the agency quietly began to embark on a program to solve the problem of the leaky booster rocket seals.[15] This shuttle seal remedy was to be systematically applied to the entire space shuttle fleet. But the redesign was not yet available for the *Challenger* flight of January 28, 1986.

So while NASA worked on solving the problem, it continued to fly, and it defined the risk as "acceptable" and "unavoidable." Dr. Alex Roland, a former NASA official, commented:

> They had put the whole future of the space program on the shuttle. There was no way out. Overwhelming problems were just denied. It wasn't conscious deception. They were kidding themselves as much as anybody else.[16]

As it turned out, this instance of groupthink had tragic consequences. The agency continued to use unsafe means to attain its ambitious goals because, as the Rogers Commission notes, they "got away with it last time." As commission member Richard Feynman commented, the decision making was

> a kind of Russian roulette. . . . [The shuttle flies with O-ring erosion] and nothing happens. Then it is suggested, therefore, that the risk is no longer so high for the next flights. We can lower our standards a little bit because we got away with it last time. . . . You got away with it, but it shouldn't be done over and over again like that.[17]

In addition to the faulty seal design, two other external sources affected the flight of the *Challenger* on January 28, 1986. One was the weather and the other was engineering data NASA received from Thiokol engineers on the night of January 27. The weather, of course, is generally a source of strain for NASA scheduling. NASA has frequently decided to delay flights because of unacceptable weather conditions. Decisions are generally resolved on the side of safety.

The weather on the night of January 27 caused a special strain at NASA directly connected to information Thiokol engineers were providing to certain NASA officials that night. Several Thiokol engineers voiced objections to the launch when they found out about the unusually cold temperature predicted for launch time the next morning. They were concerned about the detrimental effect such cold temperatures could have on the performance of the solid rocket motor joint seal, the same seal that had already generated strain at NASA. During the afternoon of January 27, Thiokol engineers presented their concerns about the cold temperatures to level III officials in the NASA readiness review process and recommended that the launch be delayed again.

The launch had already been postponed three times and scrubbed once from the planned date of January 22, 1986. Agency officials did not want to fall further behind schedule. Yet the Thiokol engineers were saying it was not safe to fly at temperatures lower than 53 degrees F, and they would not give the required launch recommendation. Engineers were told on January 27 that NASA believed it would be about 26 degrees at launch time on the 28th. (The temperature at launch was 31 degrees F.) How was this strain to be resolved?

NASA officials at level III of the readiness review were committed to launch. Another delay was unthinkable. At a teleconference between NASA and Thiokol officials, pressure was brought to bear on the Thiokol engineers to reverse their no-launch recommendation. Management officials at Thiokol also put pressure on their engineers. One Thiokol official was told to take off his engineering hat and put on his management hat. Eventually, the management at Thiokol, over the objections of some of its own engineers, gave the required recommendation for launch. The level III NASA officials did not communicate the engineering concerns about the effect of cold weather on the joint seals to levels I and II despite the earlier problems with these seals. They also recommended that the *Challenger* fly the next morning.

Rather than respond to structural strains by altering goals, it seems that level III officials altered safety standards. Two Thiokol engineers believe the latter shift was made. Both engineer Roger Boisjoly and Robert Lund, vice president for engineering, point out the different mode of thinking that occurred the night of January 27:

MR. BOISJOLY: One of my colleagues that was in the meeting summed it up best. This was a meeting where the determination was to launch, and it was up to us to prove beyond a shadow of a doubt that it was not safe to do so. This is in total reverse to what the usual is in a preflight conversation or a flight readiness review. It is usually exactly opposite that.

MR. LUND: But that evening I guess I had never had those kinds of things come from the people at Marshall. We had to prove to them that we weren't ready, and so we got ourselves in the thought process that we were trying to find some way to prove to them it wouldn't work, and we were unable to do that. We couldn't prove absolutely that the motor wouldn't work.

CHAIRMAN ROGERS: In other words, you honestly believed that you had a duty to prove that it would not work?

MR. LUND: Well, that is kind of the mode we got ourselves into that evening. It seems like we have always been in the opposite mode. I should have detected that, but I did not, but the roles kind of switched.[18]

Controls at NASA

Although NASA's organizational goals and related structural strains help us understand the events leading up to the *Challenger* flight, another factor needs to be considered. Adequate control mechanisms might still have been able to prevent the disaster.

The various investigations of the space shuttle program indicate that NASA has not been subjected to any strong supervision by an external, independent agency. Most organizations, public or private, are subjected to a variety of external mechanisms of social control. Corporations, for example, are subject to the criminal justice system, a wide variety of regulatory agencies, the media, labor unions, consumer groups, and public opinion. These external controls may be quite weak, but they guarantee at least a modest measure of vigilance.

Government agencies like NASA are subjected to far fewer controls. Congress serves as the primary watchdog, with contributions from the media and public opinion. But NASA seems to have received virtually a free ride in terms of scrutiny. This is especially true of congressional monitoring. As Robert Roe of the House Committee on Science and Technology has recently observed: "Congress has been too shy in finding fault with NASA. As a result of the *Challenger* accident, Congress and NASA must begin a new era, one in which Congress must apply the same strong oversight to NASA that it does to any other government agency." And, as Manuel Lujan, the senior Republican on the science and technology committee, has conceded: "As a committee, we may have been too trusting when NASA gave us glowing reports about the space shuttle program."[19]

As with congressional monitoring, NASA has generally been given favorable treatment in the media and held in high esteem by the public. The excitement and romance of space travel, its entertainment value, and the genuine successes of NASA have all combined to elicit media and public approval of the space agency.

Not only was no external social control exerted over NASA, apparently no adequate internal control mechanisms existed to prevent the shuttle explosion either. The organizational structure of NASA had two major control problems: (1) the reduction of the safety program and the lack of independence for safety personnel; and (2) the erosion of internal norms of safety.

In its report, the Rogers Commission devotes an entire chapter to what it calls the silent safety program at NASA. They found that the safety, reliability, and quality-assurance workforce at NASA had been reduced, and that this reduction had seriously limited NASA's capability in these vital functions. As the commission notes:

> The unrelenting pressure to meet the demands of an accelerating flight schedule might have been adequately handled by NASA if it had insisted upon the exactingly thorough procedures that were its hallmark during the *Apollo* program. An extensive and redundant safety program comprising interdependent safety, reliability, and quality-assurance functions existed during and after the lunar program to discover any potential safety problems. Between that period and 1986, however, the program became ineffective. This loss of effectiveness seriously degraded the checks and balances essential for maintaining flight safety.[20]

While the overall safety program at NASA has been reduced, a myriad of safety, reliability, and quality-assurance units remains within the overall structure. The ability of these units to act as control mechanisms, however, is seriously eroded by their lack of independence within the structure. Safety personnel are under the supervision of the very offices and units whose efforts they are to check and control. This structural flaw is described well by the Rogers Commission:

> In most cases, these organizations report to supervisors who are responsible for processing. The clear implication of such a management structure is that it fails to provide the kind of independent role necessary for flight safety. At Marshall, the director of Reliability and

Quality Assurance reports to the director of Science and Engineering who oversees the development of shuttle hardware. Again, this results in a lack of independence from the producer of hardware and is compounded by reductions in manpower, the net bringing about a decrease in effectiveness which has direct implications for flight safety.[21]

The Engineers Speak

How strongly did the Thiokol engineers speak out? The Rogers Commission provides considerable testimony regarding this issue. Robert Ebeline, manager of the ignition system and final assembly for the solid rocket motors project at Thiokol, told the commission that when it was learned that cold weather could be a problem, he convened a meeting of engineers. The meeting began at 2:30 p.m. on January 27. During the one-hour meeting, according to Ebeline, several engineers expressed serious concern about the low temperature, which they were convinced would fall far below temperatures for which the O-rings had been tested.[22]

Engineer Roger Boisjoly offered the commission a reconstruction of his and Arnold Thompson's attempt to convince the Thiokol managers of the potentially dangerous effects of cold on the O-ring seal:

> Arnie actually got up from his position which was down the table, and walked up the table and put a quarter pad down in front of the table, in front of the management folks, and tried to sketch out once again what his concern was with the [O-ring seal] joint, and when he realized he wasn't getting through, he just stopped. . . .
>
> I tried one more time with the photos. I grabbed the photos, and I went up and discussed the photos once again and tried to make the point that it was my opinion from actual observations that temperature was indeed a discriminator and we should not ignore the physical evidence that we had observed. . . . I also stopped when it was apparent that I couldn't get anybody to listen.
>
> After Arnie and I had our last say, Mr. Mason said we have to make a management decision. He turned to Bob Lund and asked him to take off his engineering hat and put on his management hat. From this point on, management formulated the points to base their decision on. There was never one comment in favor, as I have said, of launching by any engineer or other nonmanagement person in the room before or after the caucus. I was not even asked to participate in giving any input to the final decision charts. . . .

I must emphasize, I had my say, and I never [would] take [away] any management right to take the input of an engineer and then make a decision based upon that input, and I truly believe that. . . . So there was no point in me doing anything any further than I had already attempted to do. . . .

I left the room feeling badly defeated, but I felt I really did all I could to stop the launch.[23]

Of course, Boisjoly and the other engineers could have done something more. They could have gone around the level III managers and communicated their concerns directly to level II or I officials. Or, more drastically, they could have leaked their concerns to the news media. Some may believe that the Thiokol engineers had a duty to speak out, as difficult as it might have been.[24] Though hindsight tells us that speaking out might have prevented a disaster, it is doubtful that any of the engineers viewed the accident as inevitable. They might not have even viewed it as highly probable. Although Boisjoly viewed the launch as unacceptably risky, once he had communicated his concern to level III officials, he did not feel justified in challenging their right to decide by "jumping rank."

The question of under what circumstances engineers are morally justified in circumventing immediate superiors is a very difficult one to answer. Although unqualified respect for authority is not defensible, some acceptance of the right of superiors to make (even disagreeable) decisions is necessary for any functioning organization. Furthermore, saying Thiokol engineers would have been *justified* to go over the heads of the level III managers is different from saying that they had a *duty* to do so.

If Boisjoly, for example, had a duty to speak out, he can be morally faulted for not doing so. However, this judgment may be too harsh. To hold that he had a *duty* to speak out seems to presuppose that level III management officials had themselves failed to meet their moral responsibilities. Boisjoly's duty would, then, rest on the moral failure of his superiors in the organizational hierarchy. This raises the question of under what circumstances the moral failings of *others* imposes a duty on those who may be in a position to prevent the expected consequences of those failings from occurring. Boisjoly's circumstance was complicated by the fact that to prevent these consequences from occurring, he would have had to go over the heads of those he believed have the right to decide such matters. Finally, it must be acknowledged that going over the heads of the level III managers would have placed him at considerable risk of being fired or demoted. Those who go over the heads of their superiors, or "blow the whistle," typically do not fare well.[25] Although it might have been *desirable*, and even *commendable*, if Boisjoly or other engineers had spoken out, only under extraordinary circumstances do we think that we have a *duty* to take heroic measures. Whether the *Challenger* circumstances indicated such a duty is worthy of serious consideration.

Preventive Measures

In this chapter we have emphasized features of organizations that can contribute to undesirable consequences. If the harmful effects of organizations on our lives were as unavoidable as those of earthquakes, tornadoes, or hurricanes, discussing them would be pointless. But not only are organizations human constructions, they are humanly alterable.

What kinds of alternatives might reduce the chance of disasters related to our reliance on high technology, such as in the case of the *Challenger?* One conclusion that can be drawn from the *Challenger* explosion is that greater care must be exercised by those in a position to set organizational goals. External agents (such as the president, Congress, and the Pentagon) and top management must engage in serious reflection about the achievability of the goals they set. Overly ambitious and unrealistic goals should be modified or abandoned. Counterbalancing goals such as safety and the protection of the public must be given greater emphasis.

A second conclusion that can be drawn from the *Challenger* explosion is that external agents and top management need to be sensitive to the strains organizations may be subjected to when attempting to meet goals. This seems not to have been the case at NASA. Both the Reagan administration and Congress failed to provide NASA with the resources necessary to meet the flight rate goals that had been created.

Realistically, of course, organizations will always encounter strains of one kind or another as they attempt to achieve their goals. The crucial issue, therefore, is whether the organization has the ability to handle these strains without engaging in illegal or otherwise objectionable actions. It is the responsibility of top management to create and support an internal structure and culture that enables middle managers and professional staff to manage the variety of strains that are likely to occur within organizations.

Improving Communication

The key structural flaw at NASA seems to have been the lack of an effective communication system. Information flow was limited and barriers blocked a free and open exchange of vital information about matters of safety. Passing the Thiokol engineers' concerns on to levels I and II need not have compromised the decision-making powers of management. If the

level III managers' recommendation to go ahead with the launch was justifiable, the Thiokol engineers' dissent should not have swayed level I or
II managers either. Yet only level III managers were given the opportunity
to evaluate the concerns of the engineers.

Is there any reason to believe that level I or II managers would have
viewed matters differently than those at level III? In a dramatic moment at
the Rogers Commission hearings, Chairman William P. Rogers asked the
four key NASA officials to respond to a critical question:

CHAIRMAN ROGERS: By way of a question, could I ask, did any of you
gentlemen, prior to launch, know about the objections of Thiokol
to the launch?

MR. SMITH [Kennedy Space Director]: I did not.

MR. THOMAS [Launch Director]: No, sir.

MR. ALDRICH [Shuttle Program Director]: I did not.

MR. MOORE [Associate Administrator for Space Flight]: I did not.[26]

Thomas was asked what would have happened if the Thiokol concerns had
been made known to him. He replied: "I can assure you that if we had had
that information, we wouldn't have launched if it hadn't been 53 degrees."[27]

It may be tempting to place full responsibility on the level III
managers at the Marshall Space Center for failing to pass the concerns of
the Thiokol engineers on to level II. However, this is to overlook the
structural strains associated with the project that may have discouraged the
upward transmission of bad news. A basic finding of specialists in organizational communication is that bad news seldom flows up in an organization.[28] Top-level managers need to be aware of this fact and take steps to
create a climate in which all critical information—good or bad—is communicated upward.

Ironically, it was the Marshall Space Flight Center that was cited
several years ago by Philip Tompkins as having a particularly effective
communication system in its early stages.[29] Tompkins describes Werner Von
Braun's use of "Monday Notes" to find out what was happening throughout
the organization. Von Braun asked department heads to write a one-page
memo each week regarding progress, problems, and the like. They were to
arrive on Von Braun's desk each Monday morning. He would read the
memos, write comments in the margins, and send copies of all the memos
(including his notes) back to each department head. Not only was Von
Braun informed, department heads were also informed about what was

happening in other departments. Thus horizontal as well as vertical communication took place.

A very important additional advantage of this simple system was that people throughout the organization were made aware of the chief executive officer's values, moral standards, and goals. The normative environment within an organization is crucial to the control of strain. At NASA, the erosion of norms supporting the use of the safest means to accomplish organizational goals was a contributing cause of the *Challenger* accident.

The tendency to management isolation at the Marshall Space Flight Center is cited by the Rogers Commission as a major factor in the breakdown of communications at NASA. In our discussion of justificatory procedures, we pointed out the dangers of such isolation in the case of individuals. Our discussion of groupthink pointed out similar dangers in groups. Sissela Bok's test of publicity and John Rawls's original position suggest modes of reasoning that can help resist these dangers. It is interesting to speculate about what might have happened if the level III managers had tried to apply the test of publicity to the question of whether they should pass the Thiokol engineers' concerns on to higher levels.

One question they would have had to pose is this: Would the level I managers, those in whose hands the final decision rested, want to know about the engineers' concerns before approving the launch? Launch director Thomas's statement strongly suggests that the answer is yes. Even if the level III managers had been uncertain about whether Thomas would have welcomed the information, it seems that they would have had reason to pass it on. Rather than *assume* that Thomas would not be swayed by the information, given what was at stake, they should have given him the opportunity to weigh the evidence. Instead, they, in effect, decided for him.

A second question they might have posed concerns those who were to embark on the space flight. Certainly the astronauts and Christa McAuliffe knew that their mission involved risk. Did they also know that their risk taking might include launching under conditions for which critical features of the spacecraft had not been tested—and about which engineers were extremely concerned? Can it seriously be suggested that the astronauts had at least implicitly consented to this? Could this have been schoolteacher McAuliffe's understanding as well?

Nothing in the Rogers Commission report suggests that questions like these were posed by the managers at level III. Again, however, top-level managers need to let those at lower levels know that they are expected to ask such questions. Interviews with top corporate executives and middle

Figure 9.1 Shuttle Program Management Structure

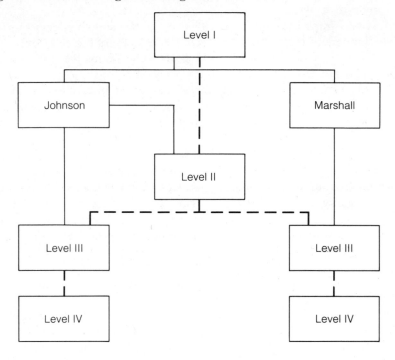

———— Institutional Chain

- — — - Program Chain

Level I:
The associate administrator for Space Flight. Oversees budgets for Johnson, Marshall, and Kennedy. Responsible for policy, budgetary, and top-level technical matters for Shuttle program.

Level II:
Manager, National Space Transportation Program. Responsible for Shuttle program baseline and requirements. Provides technical oversight on behalf of Level I.

Level III:
Program managers for Orbiter, Solid Rocket Booster, External Tank, and Space Shuttle Main Engine. Responsible for development, testing, and delivery of hardware to launch site.

Level IV:
Contractors for Shuttle elements. Responsible for design and production of hardware.

Rogers Commission Report, p. 102.

Figure 9.2 NASA's Readiness Review Levels and the Shuttle Program Management Structure

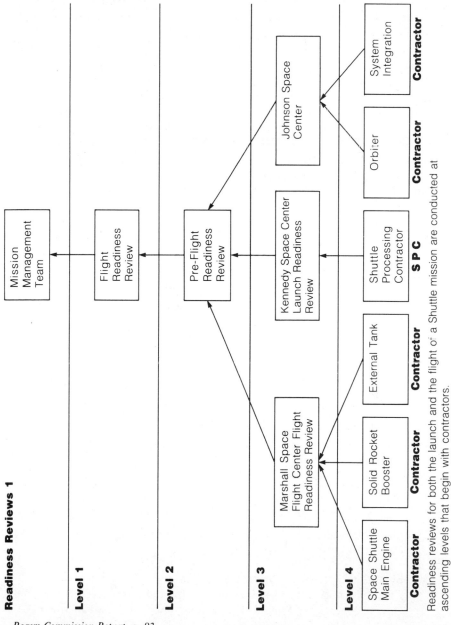

Rogers Commission Report, p. 83.

managers indicate that both groups believe that top management sets the ethical tone for the organization.[30] So top management has the main responsibility for establishing an internal environment that supports the safest possible means to achieve organizational goals, despite the structural strains that arise.

The *Challenger* accident is not a story of moral villains. No one has suggested that any individuals whose actions causally contributed to the accident had evil intentions, or that they were callously indifferent to human life. Perhaps some individuals could have (heroically) prevented the disaster. But we cannot rely only on moral individuals to make proper decisions in the use of technologies that carry enormous risks. As we have seen, these individuals are subjected to tremendous organizational pressures and constraints. A variety of external controls and monitoring mechanisms must be used if we wish to minimize the likelihood of future disasters in areas of technological risk.

Discussion Questions

1. To what extent do you think that groupthink contributed to flawed decision making in launching the Challenger? What symptoms of groupthink can you identify? What ethical problems are associated with groupthink in this case?

2. Compare and contrast the kinds of ethical problems in communication and decision making faced by individuals (a) working alone, (b) working in groups, and (c) working in large, complex organizations.

3. Would the Thiokol engineers have been justified in "blowing the whistle" prior to the Challenger launch? Did they have a moral obligation to do so?

4. Did NASA management have a moral obligation to devise and implement a more effective communication and decision-making system? Do you think that elements of Von Braun's "Monday Notes" procedure should have been continued at the Marshall Space Flight Center?

5. Should the astronauts have been informed of the fact that the O-rings had not been tested at the temperature expected under the launch conditions? Should others have been informed of the risks, including Congress and the public?

6. From an ethical perspective discuss the harmful consequences that came about as a result of the Challenger explosion, such as the loss of lives, harm to families and loved ones, impact on the public, harm to the space program, loss of confidence in a respected organization, and national security.

JEB STUART MAGRUDER: A QUESTION OF SLIPPAGE

Jeb Stuart Magruder's career beginnings were, in many respects, like those of many upwardly mobile, young American professionals.[1] In college during the 1950s he joined a fraternity, had many friends, and enjoyed an active social life. He had no particular direction in college. He graduated with a degree in political science, but he went into business because it seemed "the natural thing to do." He fell in love, married, and began raising a family. He worked hard, was ambitious, and tried a number of jobs in a short period of time. He began moving up the corporate ladder and made whatever practical moves would help him in that endeavor. He quickly discovered that it was best to cooperate, to conform, to be loyal—in short, to be a company man.

Magruder began dabbling in politics and found he enjoyed it more than business. He worked in various political campaigns and was offered a job in the Nixon administration as a reward for serving as the Southern California coordinator for the 1968 presidential campaign. Magruder accepted the job and uprooted his wife and their four children for the seventh time in their ten-year marriage.

He eagerly began his work as a special assistant to the president. Jeb Stuart Magruder felt that he had finally "made it." His assignment was to work in public relations. The Nixon administration was concerned about the poor public image the president projected. Magruder was to create the structure in the administration to deal with the problem. He reported to Bob Haldeman, special assistant to the president. Magruder was able to survive power struggles within the White House staff, but when he was asked to join the Committee for the Re-election of the President (later known as CREEP), he welcomed the opportunity to leave the White House staff and to find other means of gaining stature in the Nixon administration.

John Mitchell, attorney general of the United States, would head the campaign and Magruder would be deputy director. The campaign did not develop exactly as Magruder thought it would. He soon found himself deeply involved in many questionable campaign activities, including the bugging of the Democratic National Committee headquarters at the Watergate Hotel in Washington, D.C.

Months later he was indicted by federal investigators for his participation in the planning of the "plumbers operation," for his involvement in the cover-up, for conspiracy to obstruct justice and defraud the United States, and for eavesdropping on the Democratic headquarters. He admitted to involvement in plotting the break-in, buying equipment and hiring agents for the break-in, bugging the Democratic headquarters, impeding the Justice Department investigation by concealing the scope of the unlawful activities, influencing witnesses to give false testimony, hiding evidence, giving misleading testimony, and giving false testimony to the FBI. Magruder received reduced criminal liability because he volunteered to testify for the prosecution. Eventually he served seven months in prison.

During his testimony before the Ervin committee, Magruder spoke passionately of his friend and former ethics professor at Williams College, the Reverend William Sloane Coffin. His professor, said Magruder, had himself violated the law during an antiwar demonstration. Magruder attempted to relate his own unlawful behavior to that of his ethics professor.

Coffin, like millions of Americans, watched the Watergate proceedings on television. He expressed shock at Magruder's likening of very different kinds of lawbreakers:

> He should have known that many in the antiwar movement were protesting what they considered to be illegal laws, whose constitutionality could be tested only by a refusal to obey them. There is an enormous difference between trying to keep the nation under law and trying to keep it under Nixon, between being a loyal servant to the Constitution and being a loyal servant to the man who hires you.[2]

An interview was arranged to include Magruder, Coffin, and Studs Terkel, a well-known interviewer and author. The conversation went on for about four hours. Coffin and Terkel were curious about what happened to

Magruder along the way that led, finally, to his criminal participation in the Watergate scandal.

The conversation was published in *Harper's* magazine under the title "Reflections on a Course in Ethics: Jeb Stuart Magruder and a Question of Slippage."[3] We have reproduced substantial portions of that conversation here.

TERKEL: Why did you take that course in Ethics?

MAGRUDER: I had some problems at the time. That's how I got to know Bill. Not as a teacher, as a counselor. That's why I took his Ethics course. I related very well to Bill. He seemed to understand.

COFFIN: We were good friends. About that course in Ethics—there was nothing on civil disobedience. I was just beginning to teach and I hadn't caught on yet to the depth of complacency that would later make civil disobedience a widespread necessity. But I remember my frustration. Students were agreeing their way through life. They went to college to get accredited. This was blasphemy to me. It was a nice place, but it wasn't a challenging place—in the beautiful Berkshires, far removed from urban problems.

MAGRUDER: You used to get upset because we weren't too excited about the key issues of the day. . . .

COFFIN: I found my old grade sheet. I gave you a C.

MAGRUDER: I finished college as a good B student, despite Bill's C.

TERKEL: Do you think grades are that important?

MAGRUDER: I don't think they ever were. But I was working to get through school. I was on a scholarship. I had to borrow money from a bank—which I just finished paying off last year. I had to keep a good B average to keep my scholarship. I couldn't become a chemist or anything like that. So business was the natural thing. . . .

During my growing up, we were not particularly affluent. We were middle-income. My father had run a small printing shop, but was never as successful as he'd hoped to be. We lived a typical middle-class existence. Our values were hard work, get ahead, and do a good job. The professors in the school were interested in trying to get us on to other things. But the student body tended to be quite satisfied with life as it was.

You didn't have a broad choice. You went to law school, became a teacher, or entered business. I never thought of being a businessman. But after finishing Williams, it was the natural thing. . . .

TERKEL: Did you ever do anything at any time that offended people in authority? . . . Did you ever have what some might call dangerous thoughts?

MAGRUDER: I'm not really sure what dangerous thoughts are. I found that in the corporate life and in the government it's best to do what your superiors want—as long as it's within ethical and legal limits. I was very strong on that. I used to tell people who worked for me at the Committee to Re-elect: You've got to do what the hierarchy wants, that's why you're here. In the corporate life, you must conform or it can be very difficult.

There were a couple of occasions during my business career where I didn't follow the prescription. This hurt. I had a couple of setbacks that wouldn't have occurred if I had conformed.

I was at Jewel Tea in Chicago and doing very well. I had been advertising and then merchandising manager of one of their divisions. When a job offer came from California, I took it. It was a mistake and I decided to go back to Jewel. They agreed. I changed my mind again. Jewel was very upset with me, and correctly so. After that I made up my mind: I'd better toe the line for people employing me.

COFFIN: It must have been quite a shock to discover your team wasn't the team you thought it was—Haldeman or Ehrlichman, taping your conversations.

MAGRUDER: I must admit internally I was bothered by the fact that people I considered good friends were taping conversations without my knowledge. I was surprised. It wasn't an adversary relationship. There was no need to tape.

Other than that, I haven't been bothered by any of the accusations, charges, and countercharges. I understand the process by which individuals defend their positions. . . .

COFFIN: Do you accept that as part of the game? Each one survives his own way, even though the guy may have been your buddy?

MAGRUDER: I don't like it, but I accept it. My philosophy is: If you can't do anything about it, don't worry about it. Internally it bothers me. . . .

COFFIN: You developed a stronger internal drive than I remember at Williams.

MAGRUDER (*Acknowledges observation*): . . . A lot of people that worked with me at the White House had a similar kind of aggressiveness, ambition. They were more interested in power than money, more interested in getting things done. Not just talking about them. I became one of these people when I finished Williams. I wanted to accomplish things, get things done. Not just for the sake of getting them done—but there was something in that, too.

I decided not to follow the path of my peers, to stay in business, move up the ladder and become the president of a company. . . . Politics was much more exciting than business. You're working for a man instead of a product. Money alone wasn't the secret of success. During my work at the White House, you had many well-to-do people coming to you asking for your guidance. Even though they had far more wealth than any of us. People would be catering to you. They were attracted to the power that the White House exuded.

COFFIN: This helps explain Watergate, too, doesn't it? You told me Watergate was inevitable. You were disturbed by widespread business practices, the way America operates.

MAGRUDER: I would never say the country caused Watergate. Specific individuals are to blame. But there are certain values, certain characteristics and habits in this country—a desire to get ahead, impatience. Our overwhelming legal structure creates in the average businessman, the average worker, a feeling that he has to do his share of shaving, whether it be on his income tax or on his expense account.

Sometimes you just go along. There were decisions the president made that I didn't agree with. But since he was president and I was an aide, it wasn't something I should do anything about. If you're very much against a policy, you should resign. Once it's made, you should go along. . . .

There were disagreements with the staff. But we all felt since we're not in the decision-making process, it was appropriate to follow the policies the president set. You could disagree privately, but not publicly.

COFFIN: Did that trouble you?

MAGRUDER: I subverted my personal feelings to what I felt was the president's desire. I think that's the root cause of Watergate.

COFFIN: Why was loyalty to the boss so important?

MAGRUDER: . . . The presidency more than a corporation or a university breeds a certain necessity for loyalty. Personal loyalty to the man as against the office.

At the university you can sit and discuss alternatives. But if you're working at the White House, you enjoy your job, you've got four children, you're not rich—sure, you can leave and go somewhere else. But is it that important? So you subvert individual judgment over here to gain a more effective policy over there. It's the same in business.

COFFIN: When you subvert your opinion, you are in effect subverting yourself. Your identity is at the mercy of the person to whom you're loyal. Right?

MAGRUDER: That's true. You can't work in any structured situation without having this subversion going on on a daily basis. Most of the cases I can think of—with the exception of the war—were not great moral issues. They were practical issues. . . .

COFFIN: What has disturbed you most in all these revelations?

MAGRUDER: The tapping. I was dealing with the senior staff people at the White House in good faith and they disappointed me.

COFFIN: What upset you was that you sacrificed a good deal of yourself for loyalty. And the loyalty you gave was not returned.

MAGRUDER: It wasn't that Haldeman didn't trust me. It was that he was using me. That disturbed me more than anything else. It's a personal feeling. A feeling of hurt.

COFFIN: This affects you more than the revelation of the 3,000-some sorties over Cambodia?

MAGRUDER: I'm disturbed by that, the lying and so on. It's inexcusable. And the bombing of the civilian population. But the tapping is so personal. Most of us are affected by what we can directly relate to. It's natural. If I were in a village in Cambodia, I'd be more concerned about the bombing. But . . .

COFFIN: Loyalty to a person can distort a larger loyalty. . . . There's a larger loyalty than a personal loyalty to the boss.

MAGRUDER: . . . There is nothing I can say to justify the use of wiretaps in the Democratic headquarters. At the time, it wasn't important. The campaign was important. The reelection was the prevailing ethos at the camp. . . .

There's a growing body of opinion in this country that believes wiretapping is quite typical and American. The government does it, private investigators do. A common, harmless practice. Now I understand someone's desire not to have his phone tapped. I know what's it's like.

COFFIN: If you start giving away your right to say no, there's an erosion of self. If Watergate's inevitable, it's because life is consequential. One thing leads to another.

MAGRUDER: It's a question of slippage. I sort of slipped right into it. Each act you take leads you to the next act, and eventually you end up with a Watergate. It's very typical in large corporations. Someone else is influential. He has an idea and he gets the idea approved. You're the one who has to carry it out. You don't agree with it, but it's important to satisfy the group consensus: "It isn't that important and I might as well go along."

COFFIN: . . . It sounds as if you're loyal because you're afraid of losing your position in the power structure.

MAGRUDER: It's very difficult to set your own standard and continue in the power structure. I always felt I could do more by staying in the system. Maybe that's just the way of satisfying my conscience. I wanted to stay with the government for the next four years, but I was determined to get out of the White House and into an agency where I'd have more independence. I followed instructions and did things I did not agree with because it was important for my personal success—and also for the good of the president.

COFFIN: It's interesting how slippage occurs. It starts as a matter of public relations. You justify it in the name of national security. And what comes out is blatant lying. It starts as a small misrepresentation, by the way in which you package your product. . . .

MAGRUDER: Truth has now become my best product. There's a world of difference today than before I decided to tell the truth. I feel comfortable.

COFFIN: Sure. Lying to cover up is a reflex of insecurity. And public relations is sometimes its handmaiden.

MAGRUDER: . . . [Y]ou've got to go back to '70. When planning started for the campaign, these activities seemed important. By the time it wasn't important, it was too late to change. Once plans get into motion, you rarely stop them.

COFFIN: An individual could.

MAGRUDER: An individual could? That's a good point. I could have stopped Liddy. But Liddy was more dedicated to achieving his ends than I was concerned about what he was doing. You're absolutely right. But other people interacted and thought it was best for him to stay. Because it wasn't that important to me. I didn't stand my ground. I should have.

TERKEL: You were doing what a successful young corporate executive would do today. . . .

Where are the heroes of yesteryear? You say it's tough to find one today. What about John Mitchell?

MAGRUDER: He was a hero to me, no question about it. I still have a tremendous affection for him. He treated me well. I found him fair and above board in all his dealings. Unlike his public image. He's one of the finest people I've known. What's happened doesn't change that. If you discarded someone because he had disappointed you, you wouldn't be much of a friend.

In the year and a half I worked for him, I thought most of his decisions were excellent. He has an excellent mind. I didn't agree with all his activities as Attorney General. He certainly was not a civil libertarian. But on a personal note, he was a very fine person to work for. If you said, "My wife's not feeling well, I'd like to leave early," he'd say, "Jeb, leave right now." At the White House, this was not a typical response to personal problems. He was more of a father than a boss. He's a hero to me, as much as any person my age has heroes.

COFFIN: That's what bothers me, Jeb—the littleness of loyalties, at the expense of great loyalties. We're talking about an Attorney General, a man sworn to uphold the Constitution of the United States, a man who came in with banners flying for law and order.

MAGRUDER: Well, as a human being, and hopefully as a Christian, I can't turn my back on a friend. You don't want me to turn my back on people. I'm no better or worse. We've all sinned at one time or another. I'm not going to throw stones.

COFFIN: I'm not asking you to throw stones or turn your back on people. One can have a great compassion for the sinner without condoning his sin. But I'm wondering whether you feel this whole experience was incredibly belittling. We're talking about a country, the most powerful in the world, and you're talking about loyalty to the boss. He was kind and let you take the afternoon off when your wife was sick. But he didn't hesitate to fool around with the Constitution when it suited his aims. What bothers me terribly are the consequences of this whole affair. It's one thing to say he doesn't beat his wife, he's a good fellow. But, if by his actions he belittles his country, that's something else. But perhaps in public and in private life we get what we deserve to a much larger degree than we want to admit. . . .

What concerns me pastorally is that I sense in you a great need to be honest. But your capacity for honesty has been eroded by this experience. In the same way, many people sense a need to love, but have lost their capacity to love. These things gradually erode human beings so that they're really not that deeply human anymore. What disturbs me most about Watergate is that the failure lay in being caught. It's not the truth that has set people free. They're still prisoners of their falsehood. It's only that they were caught. There still hasn't been a confrontation with the truth. . . .

Power can destroy an individual's capacity to think big, to think imaginatively, to feel deeply about others who are in desperate need. I think your experience eroded those qualities you had while you were at Williams. You just had a bad experience, and it will take a long time to recover what it has cost you in terms of your humanity.

MAGRUDER: I'm going to try to change my lifestyle. I'll probably try to teach. I'd like to teach Government. I think it could be invaluable to the students because I was there and I knew what it was. . . .

I think it's impossible to change one's view without taking the time to examine what it really is. I haven't done that yet. The last 20 years all I've done is kept moving up the ladder, working very hard to make sure I was going up that ladder. Now I finally have some time to go inside me, to find out why I did certain things. But I can't erase 20 years of activity and conscious thought just like that. I think much of what the administration did is beneficial. Some of our policies had purely political bases. We didn't spend time on the disadvantaged for the simple reason that there were no votes there. That's not a good reason. But for the most part, our policies were based on deeply held beliefs. We tried to break down the bureaucracy as an overgrown instrument of totalitarianism. . . .

The true democracy is where the individual is able to affect his own situation. That is not true in this country anymore. The big lobbies can do it, but the individual can't. People feel they have no influence. So if you don't feel you have any interest, you don't worry about it. You just go along.

TERKEL: When you're an old, old man and finally die, your epitaph might read: He was easy to get along with.

MAGRUDER (*Laughs*): That's true. That's what Bill said about me.

COFFIN: . . . It can be turned to the good. "He's easy to get along with" has been your way of just sliding around. . . .

To be Jeb is terribly valuable at this moment. His experience has been an all-American one. His change could be an all-American one. We're not naturally profound. We usually have to be forced down, forced by failure. In my own life, I've learned far more from my failures than I have from my successes. If Jeb can confront these failures with honesty, it will be healthy for many, because his experience is the experience of almost all of us. The slippage and sliding and shaving and loyalties that are too small and the need to be on the team—if all this gets examined and put before the American public, it can be terribly useful. The greatest tragedy for Jeb would be to have the experience and miss the meaning. . . .

The possibilities of Americans seeing themselves in the life and times of Jeb Magruder could be very helpful.

MAGRUDER: Well, I think it would be a greater tragedy than the Watergate affair itself if people didn't learn from our experience.

Magruder did choose to look more deeply into his Watergate experience in his book *Jeb Stuart Magruder: An American Life—One Man's Road to Watergate*. In the closing pages, Magruder addresses himself to a frequently asked question about whether a flaw in his character accounted for his Watergate misdeeds.

Obviously, someone who knowingly breaks the law has some flaw of character or of judgment or of sensitivity to right and wrong. Yet I think, too, that if we consider how many people broke the law in the Watergate affair, men who were usually model citizens in their private lives, we must ask if our failures do not somehow reflect larger failures in the values of our society.

I think that, as Bill Coffin suggested, I am a fairly representative member of my generation, and, looking back over my life, I think that I and many members of my generation placed far too much emphasis on our personal ambitions, on achieving success, as measured in materialistic terms, and far too little emphasis on moral and humanistic values. I think that most of us who were involved in Watergate were unprepared for the pressures and temptations that await you at the highest levels of the political world. We had private morality but not a sense of public morality. Instead of applying our private morality to public affairs, we accepted the President's standards of political behavior, and the results were tragic for him and for us.[4]

Magruder also discusses his shame and sorrow for what he had done. He addresses specifically the personal harm to himself, his family, his cause, and society as a whole as a result of his involvement in Watergate:

> I have described many things I did that I'm now deeply ashamed of. I've tried to relate them candidly, and I've not attempted, as I detailed each wrongdoing, to express to the reader my retrospective shame and sorrow. But the reader is assured that there has been a great deal of shame and sorrow. I've damaged my own life, I've hurt those I love most, and I've helped deal a terrible blow to the political cause I believe in. I hope that young people who are in politics, or who may enter politics, may view this book as a cautionary tale. I won't tell them . . . to stay away from politics. I would tell them, rather, to play the game hard but clean, and to bring to public life the same high standards they would apply in private life. I didn't do that, and I feel that I owe an apology to the American people for having abused the position of public trust that I was given.[5]

In his closing thoughts, Magruder relates his sense of personal imprisonment even before receiving his sentence. And, in retrospect, he seems already to be beginning to find ways to atone for his wrongs and to reshape his life in more positive, socially useful ways:

> As I write this, it appears that Judge Sirica will soon pass sentence on me. I wouldn't be honest if I said I expect to benefit from prison. If I never went to prison, I would have been changed by this experience. I've been living in a kind of prison for almost two years, ever since the day the burglars were arrested in the Watergate. Yet if society's laws are to be respected, people who break them must be punished, and prison is one tangible form of punishment. I hope that my prison term will, in society's eyes, wipe my record clean and give me a chance to start anew. As I told the senators, I don't intend to be destroyed by this experience. I will still have a long life ahead of me, and I think it can be a good life, for me and my family.[6]

Jeb Stuart Magruder served his seven months in prison and later earned a theology degree from the Princeton Theological Seminary. He became an ordained minister and was assigned to a parish in the eastern part of the United States. Later he moved to Columbus, Ohio, as an ordained minister.

Magruder moved into adulthood as many other Americans do—by attending college and earning a degree. His college experience seems to have been similar to that of many others—no specific burning ambition, no clear-cut professional aspirations. He entered the workforce, became determined to get ahead, and learned quickly that it paid to be loyal and obedient.

In the Nixon White House, loyalty was expected and rewarded. Authority was to be unquestioned. Anyone who deviated from this norm could expect sanctions or dismissal. The power of Haldeman and Ehrlichman was well known and blatantly applied. The power of the presidency was obvious and permeated the environment Magruder worked in.

Practical efficiency was a prime value in the Nixon campaign. Things simply had to get done. The president had to be reelected. Everyone was expected to cooperate to get the job accomplished.

Magruder admits that he really did not see the implications of many of the things he was asked to do. His failure to understand the significance of what he was doing at the time soon became his downfall. As he cooperated, he discovered that it became easier to lie, to break the law, to participate in the cover-up, and so on. A subtle, gradual erosion of his moral character occurred. As he puts it: "It's a matter of slippage. I sort of slipped right into it. Each act leads you to the next act, and eventually you end up with a Watergate."

It was not until the Watergate burglars were caught that he began to question the morality of what he had been doing. And it was not until criminal charges were made that he came forward and began telling the truth as he knew it.

The story of Jeb Stuart Magruder and Watergate is an American tragedy. Despite the fact that Magruder was able to redirect his life after prison, he suffered in many ways from the entire affair, especially morally. His family and friends were harmed. The institution of the presidency was harmed. Confidence in government and the democratic process was weakened. Careers were destroyed. We still feel the ill effects of Watergate today.

As we reflect on all of this, we may feel uneasy, because Magruder is so much like us. We must ask how much of the younger Magruder is in each of us. Magruder hopes that we will learn from his experiences. His story personalizes Watergate, helps us to understand why it happened, and makes us wonder how we might have responded, given similar opportunities and subjected to similar pressures. And it may prod us to ask whether we are ready to deal with the little "Watergates" we may someday have to face.

Discussion Questions

1. What kinds of excuses did Magruder give for his involvement in the Watergate break-in and subsequent cover-up? How well do they stand up to the test of publicity?

2. Review the kinds of moral reasoning identified in Lawrence Kohlberg's theory of moral development (Chapter 4). To what extent can Magruder's various attempts to justify or excuse his behavior be characterized in terms of Kohlberg's account?

3. Review the Hastings Center objectives for courses in ethics (Chapter 1). To what extent do you think that Coffin's ethics course succeeded in helping Magruder meet these objectives after he left Williams College?

4. Magruder says, "It's a question of slippage. I sort of slipped right into it. Each act you take leads you to the next act, and eventually you end up with a Watergate." Explain and comment on this statement.

5. Discuss Coffin's statement: "What concerns me pastorally is that I sense in you a great need to be honest. But your capacity for honesty has been eroded by this experience."

6. Examine Magruder's statements about wiretapping conversations. Are they consistent? To what extent do they exhibit golden rule reasoning?

7. Can you find examples of egocentric thinking on Magruder's part?

8. To what extent does groupthink seem to have played a role in Magruder's involvement in Watergate?

9. Magruder says, "I think that, as Bill Coffin suggested, I am a fairly representative member of my generation." Do you think this is an accurate observation? Why or why not?

10. Magruder acknowledges that he could have stopped Liddy. How might he have done this? Did he have a moral obligation to do it? Explain.

11. What do you think Coffin means when he says that there was no confrontation of truth by the Watergate participants?

12. Discuss Terkel's statement to Magruder: "When you're an old, old man and finally die, your epitaph might read: He was easy to get along with." To what extent do you agree that this would be an apt epitaph? In what sense is this a criticism of Magruder?

13. Discuss Magruder's statement: "We had private morality but not a sense of public morality. Instead of applying our private morality to public affairs, we accepted the president's standards of political behavior, and the results were tragic for him and for us." What should be the relationship between public and private morality?

14. Discuss the loyalties that concerned Magruder: loyalty to his boss, Mitchell; loyalty to the president; loyalty to the country and the Constitution; loyalty to his wife and children. How might these be related to living up to his own principles or maintaining his self-respect?

15. With which position are you most likely to agree: that young people should stay away from politics, or that they should "play the game hard but clean" and bring to public life the same high standards they would apply to private life? Explain. Discuss this kind of issue as it might arise in other areas, such as law, medicine, teaching, business, or nongovernmental public relations.

CANDOR AND CONFIDENTIALITY

When a player says something, do I know if he means it? My coaches ask if they should say something to correct the guy. I say, no, don't do that, because you'll undress him. Tell him what you think and that man will be done forever.

You must always allow a man to keep his dignity. I always say the hardest thing is truthfully not to tell the truth on that subject.

—Sparky Anderson, manager of the Detroit Tigers[1]

Sissela Bok's *principle of veracity* holds that a moral presumption against lying exists. This is not the same as saying that a presumption in favor of disclosing the truth exists. In some kinds of situations, such a presumption may exist. We may claim rights to be informed about our medical condition by our doctors, hazards in our workplace by our employers, or dangers of consumer products by manufacturers. Only recently has acknowledgment of these rights become general, and even now their extent is widely debated. In any case, the failure to respect a person's right to know something need not involve lying, or even deliberate deception. It can be the result of indifference, oversight, or negligence. But in the absence of some sort of right to know, it cannot be assumed that, in general, not disclosing information is objectionable.

Whether or not one should be candid is largely a matter of *discretion*. In some situations it may be quite clear that candor is called for. For example, suppose a student has been doing failing work in a class and the deadline for dropping classes is drawing near. If the student asks the professor whether, if through hard work, he has a reasonable chance of getting a C by the end of the semester, he is entitled to a candid appraisal.

However, candor sometimes betrays insensitivity. Saying nothing at all about someone's new living room furnishings may be preferable to volunteering, "I think the decor in your living room is tasteless and dull." An indiscriminate gossip can be very candid, but quite indiscreet. Simply speaking out truthfully about what we know can cause needless harm or suffering. It can also betray confidences or show a lack of respect for individual privacy.

Confidentiality poses special problems. At the personal level, maintaining confidentiality respects the right of individuals to share private matters only with others of their own choosing. As Sissela Bok points out, some degree of control over who knows about our thoughts, plans, and actions is necessary for guarding ourselves against exploitation and danger; it is also essential for our privacy and self-esteem.[2] This is, fundamentally, a matter of individual *autonomy*.

But individual autonomy should not be understood independently of meaningful *relationships* between individuals. If controlling access to the private areas of one's life can be accomplished only by keeping them entirely to oneself, interpersonal relationships will be severely restricted. Regard for relationships between individuals requires an acknowledgment of the right to share private thoughts, aspirations, and plans.

The Burden of Secrecy

Respect for confidentiality at the personal level can be further solidified by promises or pledges to keep matters confidential. Such explicit commitments place trust in the integrity of those who make them. At the same time, these promises or pledges can strengthen bonds between individuals.

However, some cautions should be noted. Confidential information places a moral burden on those who receive it, so those who pass it on should do so with care. How should sharing secrets be handled? Sometimes it goes like this. Greg divulges something to Roger and then adds, "Of course, I'd like you to keep this confidential between us." The problem is that Roger was given no advance warning that what he was about to hear is confidential. Greg has put Roger on the spot. Since there is a moral presumption in favor of respecting confidentiality, Greg has attempted unilaterally to impose an obligation on Roger. Roger may wish that he had not been told anything about the matter. He will now have to take up the burden of not sharing what he has learned with others who may want him to share it with them. Or he may not agree that it ought to be kept confidential. Either way, Roger is in a morally uncomfortable situation. We would suggest that those who wish to share confidences give careful thought to whether they may be imposing an unwelcome moral burden on others.

This problem is only partially resolved if Greg first asks Roger if he will keep confidential what Greg wants to share with him. Not knowing what he is about to hear, Roger might not know whether it ought to be kept confidential. So he must weigh the moral risk of promising to keep unknown matters confidential.

No general solution to these problems presents itself. Again, moral discretion rather than a reliance on rigid rules seems called for. Moral discretion requires one to try to take into account the morally relevant factors, applying the tests of universalizability and reversibility. The test of publicity is as relevant here as in the evaluation of lies. This is so whether one is trying to decide whether to share something confidential with another or one is trying to decide whether to treat what one has heard as confidential.

We offer two more cautions. Although we agree that there is a moral presumption against breaches of confidentiality, determining just what is a truly confidential matter can be difficult to determine. On the one hand, indicating that one wishes something to be kept confidential sometimes suffices for its being a confidential matter. But *saying* that something is confidential does not necessarily make it so. It may be the case that some things that one wishes to keep private should not be. This is especially true in professional and business situations, but it can also happen at the personal level. On the other hand, *not* saying that something is confidential does not necessarily mean that it is not. Often an understanding that what is being said should be treated confidentially is assumed. Again, no general rules can replace sensitivity and judgment.

Professional Discretion

Confidentiality is fundamental to many relationships, particularly between professionals and their clients. Without assurances of confidentiality, patients would be more likely to withhold information from doctors that is necessary to adequate medical care. Clients who withhold information from their lawyers impair the ability of lawyers to provide legal services that protect the rights of clients. When clients are businesses, they may suffer competitively if their professional consultants divulge confidential information to others. And, of course, employees of businesses or other organizations can cause serious harm by divulging confidential information (for example, trade secrets) to others.

The question of when, if ever, the obligation to respect confidentiality between professionals and clients may be overridden is the subject of much controversy. The legal profession has been divided about whether lawyers have the right to disclose that their clients have told them that they plan to commit a crime. The American Bar Association's Model Code of Professional Responsibility, for example, now permits (not requires) lawyers to disclose their clients' plans to commit crimes that pose an imminent threat to human life. But despite the recent protests of many lawyers, it does not permit disclosure of clients' plans to defraud others of huge amounts of money.[3] On the other hand, the Supreme Court recently concluded that a defendant's constitutional rights were not violated by his lawyer's threat to expose him if he perjured himself on the witness stand in his murder trial.[4] And in the famous *Tarasoff* case, the California Supreme Court found against a psychiatrist who failed to warn a murder victim of violent threats his client had made toward her. The court concluded, "The protective privilege ends where the public peril begins."[5]

Of course, even if professional codes and legal decisions were to draw reasonably clear guidelines, moral questions might remain. Professional codes themselves need to be morally evaluated. Some lawyers, for example, might find some parts of the ABA code so morally inadequate that they are prepared to violate them—on moral grounds. Unless *moral* is to be equated with the provisions of one's professional code, the possibility of justifiable departures must be taken seriously. Similar considerations apply to legal decisions. While professional codes and legal determinations themselves may carry considerable moral weight, they do not justify blind acceptance.

The Job Candidate

Janice Jordan works for a public university that has advertised nationally for a new associate dean. She learns that an old acquaintance is one of the final candidates who have been invited for on-site interviews. At first Janice is excited and pleased. She has always thought highly of her acquaintance. Then one of her colleagues tells her: "Don't get too excited about your friend's candidacy. I've heard that it's really all settled. It's an inside hire—Jack's the one they want. They're just going through the motions with external candidates, you know. We have to look good in the affirmative-action area. Your friend makes us look good because she's a woman." Janice is not sure that her colleague's statement is true. So she asks some other colleagues what they think. They basically agree. What finally convinces her, however, is a conversation she overhears between two members of the selection committee. One member says: "I wish we could just hire Jack without going through all this external-search nonsense. We all know that Jack's the one we're going to hire anyway." The other replies: "I agree. Bringing in these candidates is a waste of our time. But I guess we have to do it to satisfy the affirmative-action folks."

Janice finds this situation very disturbing. She feels sorry for the external candidates, especially her old acquaintance. Somehow, she thinks, it's all terribly unfair. She is also angry that affirmative action is not being taken more seriously.

Discussion Questions

1. Should Janice say anything to her colleagues about what she thinks? If so, what (and how)?

2. Should Janice say anything to the members of the selection committee after she overhears their conversation? If so, what (and how)?

3. Should Janice say anything to her old acquaintance? (Does it matter how close they are?) If so, what (and how)?

4. Is there anyone else Janice should discuss this situation with? If so, how should she approach it?

CAS Manufacturing

Laura Talbot has been employed at CAS Manufacturing for nearly 15 years. During that time she has steadily moved up the ladder. Now she is head researcher in a special products division. She is very happy working for CAS and likes the community where she lives. In fact, she would be perfectly content to work at CAS until retirement. In addition, she feels a strong sense of loyalty to CAS and is proud of the consistent contribution her division has made to the success of CAS. It also seems that management is happy with Laura and her division, too. Each year Laura's division receives high commendation, and division employees receive frequent, substantial merit-pay increases.

However, a complication has arisen for Laura. She has been offered a very attractive position at a firm in another town. She has sought the advice of several of her good friends, including you.

Meanwhile, you have been serving on the long-range-planning committee for CAS. Although no definite plans have been formulated, the president of CAS has indicated to your committee that to increase profits, CAS is contemplating a dramatic shift of resources. This shift would involve eliminating some of CAS's divisions— possibly some that are now quite productive. Laura's division is on the list of those that might be eliminated. The president has reassured your committee that only some of the divisions listed would have to be eliminated. So he has instructed the committee that the matter be kept strictly confidential so that employee morale is not needlessly affected by what, at present, can be only highly speculative. The spreading of rumors, warned the president, can serve no constructive purpose, and it can cause needless worry for those employees whose jobs will not actually be affected.

Laura has to decide about the job offer within the next three days. Since the president will be out of the country for the next two weeks (vacationing and contemplating the future of CAS), neither you nor Laura has time to consult with him.

Discussion Questions

1. What do you say when Laura approaches you and asks: "This job offer looks awfully attractive—it's a booming company, and it promises opportunities for rapid advancement. But I really like it here, too. How do things look to you at CAS? What do you think I can expect from CAS down the road?"

2. To what extent, if any, do you think your answer to Laura should be affected by your close friendship? What if you and Laura were not friends at all? What if you disliked her?
3. Do you think the president's position is justified? Is it paternalistic?
4. What do you think are the major ethical issues raised by this situation?

Confidences and Consequences

Part I: Keeping Confidences

Harry is president of the local division of Tiforp, Inc. He has just been informed by national headquarters that his division will be moved within a year. He must consult with headquarters about plans for relocating or releasing employees. He is told to submit his recommendations within the next 30 days. Meanwhile, he is told that the move is confidential. Headquarters does not want the move announced until plans have been finalized.

Harry confides in his wife Mary.

Mary has a close relationship with Alice and tells her of the impending change, emphasizing that the information is confidential.

Alice is best friends with Betty, whose husband Oscar works for the local division of Tiforp. Alice knows that Betty and Oscar are within days of deciding to buy an expensive new house in the area. Alice concludes that they have a right to know what is happening at Tiforp. So she tells Betty.

Discussion Questions

1. Should Harry have told Mary about Tiforp's plans? In general, is it all right for spouses to share such confidential information?
2. Should Mary have told Alice?
3. Once Alice learns about the situation, is she, too, bound by obligations of confidentiality?
4. Was Alice justified in telling Betty?
5. Would Betty be justified in telling her husband? Would this involve any breach of confidentiality on her part?

Part II. The Consequences

Unknown to Mary and Alice, Harry and Oscar have disliked each other intensely for a long time. When Oscar hears the news from Betty, he is furious. He wants to confront Harry directly. But he is afraid he will get fired on the spot. So instead, he takes some other employees into his confidence. He is quite sure they will spread the word. Within two days, a group of employees then confront Harry and ask him what is going on.

Discussion Questions

1. Should Oscar have directly confronted Harry rather than doing what he did?
2. Did Oscar have any obligation of confidentiality, given the way he acquired the information? Did he have any other responsibilities concerning what to do with the information?
3. Did any of the workers have any obligation of confidentiality, given the way they acquired the information? Did they have any other responsibilities concerning what to do with the information?

Part III: The Reply

When confronted, Harry replies: "This is news to me! Somebody around here's obviously trying to stir things up. I'd like to know who the jerk is. Who told you this, anyway?" Evaluate Harry's reply.

Notes

Chapter One

1. *Doonesbury*, *Kalamazoo Gazette*, Sept. 1, 1975.
2. *Doonesbury*, *Kalamazoo Gazette*, Sept. 2–3, 1975.
3. *Mad*. © 1979 by E. C. Publications, Inc. Used by permission of *Mad* Magazine.
4. Frank Chapman Sharp and Phillip G. Fox, *Business Ethics* (New York: Appleton-Century-Crofts, 1937), p. 3. Cited in Marcus G. Singer, ed., *Morals and Values* (New York: Scribners, 1977), pp. 21–22.
5. Samuel Florman, "Moral Blueprints," *Harper's*, October 1978, p. 31.
6. Plato, *The Trial and Death of Socrates*, trans. G.M.A. Grube (Hackett, 1975), p. 20.
7. Ibid., p. 33.
8. Daniel Callahan, "Goals in the Teaching of Ethics," in *Ethics Teaching in Higher Education*, ed. Daniel Callahan and Sissela Bok. A Hastings Center Monograph (New York: Plenum, 1980), pp. 61–74. Used with permission of Daniel Callahan, The Hastings Center. Callahan lists a fifth goal: eliciting a sense of obligation. We agree with this goal (although we prefer *responsibility* to *obligation*). It seems to us, however, that this goal is implicit in the accounts of the first two goals.
9. John Dean, *Blind Ambition* (New York: Simon & Schuster, 1976).
10. Presented by Roy V. Hughson and Philip M. Kohn in *Chemical Engineering*, May 5, 1980, pp. 100–107.
11. See Thomas Murray, "Learning to Deceive," *Hastings Center Reports*, April 1980, pp. 11–14.
12. This example was presented by James Taylor of Notre Dame University to a group of engineers and professional philosophers for discussion.
13. This is a contemporary version of a story presented by Myron Tibus in "The Engineer and Public Policy-Making," in *Ethical Problems in Engineering*, ed. Robert Baum and Al Flores (Troy, N.Y.: RPI, 1980), p. 249. The updated version was presented by Harold Shapiro, then president of the University of Michigan, in Kalamazoo, Michigan, in a talk on the relationship between business and society.

Chapter Two

1. Bok, *Lying*, p. xiii. Reprinted by permission of Pantheon Books, a division of Random House, Inc.
2. Ibid., p. 180.
3. *Newsweek*, May 5, 1986, p. 17.
4. "The Legacy of Watergate," *Newsweek*, June 14, 1982, p. 36.
5. Ibid., p. 38.
6. Ibid., p. 36.
7. Ibid., p. 37.
8. "Americans Distrust Their Leaders," *USA Today*, Vol. 107, No. 2407, April 1979, 2.
9. Thomas Nilsen discusses the idea of "significant choice" in his *Ethics in Speech Communication* (Indianapolis: Bobbs-Merrill, 1966).
10. "Legacy of Watergate," p. 36.
11. Ibid., p. 37.
12. Ibid., p. 39.

13. Ibid., p. 40.

14. Ibid.

15. "Hostages Release Is Linked to Shift in Iran Policy," *New York Times*, Nov. 4, 1986, p. 1.

16. *Newsweek*, Dec. 1, 1986, p. 26.

17. At this writing, Congress is in the midst of its hearings. It will be a long time before the full story on the Iran-Contra affair is known.

18. *Newsweek*, Mar. 9, 1987, p. 16.

19. Ibid., p. 19.

20. *Newsweek*, Dec. 15, 1986, p. 28.

21. Information in this paragraph is drawn from *Newsweek*, July 6–Aug. 10, 1987.

22. ABC News Poll, ABC News *World News This Morning*, Aug. 7, 1987.

23. "Still No Smoking Gun," *Newsweek*, Aug. 10, 1987, p. 12.

24. NCB *Today Show*, Aug. 13, 1987.

25. Ibid.

26. "More Confidence in Leadership," *Current Opinion* 5, no. 4 (April 1977): 37.

27. *The Connecticut Mutual Report on American Values in the '80s: The Impact of Belief*, 1981 (prepared by the Connecticut Mutual Life Insurance Company, Hartford; the survey was conducted by Research and Forecasts, Inc.), p. 27.

28. "Codes of Ethics in Corporations and Trade Associations and the Teaching of Ethics in Graduate Business Schools," a survey conducted for Ethics Resource Center, Opinion Research Corporation, Princeton, New Jersey, June 1979, p. 14.

29. *U.S. News & World Report*, Feb. 23, 1987, p. 54. References to this article are used by permission of *U.S. News & World Report*.

30. Ibid.

31. Ibid., p. 59.

32. Ibid., p. 60.

33. Ibid., p. 55.

34. Ibid.

35. Case based on Lidia Wasowicz, "Cheating: Newest U.S. Fad," *Detroit Free Press*, Aug. 30, 1983, p. 15A. Copyright 1983. Reprinted by permission of United Press International.

36. Case based on James Litke, "Ann Landers Says 'Recycling' Ended," *Kalamazoo Gazette*, May 3, 1982. Reprinted by permission of the Associated Press.

37. Case based on David K. Shipler, "Spokesman Quits State Dept. Post on Deception Issue," *New York Times*, Oct. 9, 1986, p. 1.

38. Case based on Ibid. and Bernard Weinraub, "The Ex-Spokesman: Bernard Kalb," *New York Times*, Oct. 9, 1986, p. A-16.

Chapter Three

1. Kenneth Andersen, *Persuasion: Theory and Practice*, 2nd ed. (Boston: Allyn and Bacon, 1978), p. 7.

2. Ibid., p. 3.

3. Ibid., p. 21.

4. Lester Thonssen and A. Craig Baird, *Speech Criticism* (New York: Ronald Press, 1948), p. 448.

5. Quintilian, *Institutes of Oratory*, trans. J. S. Watson (London, 1856).

6. Andersen, p. 21. See also Andersen, "A Code of Ethics for Speech Communication," *Spectra* 20, no. 1 (January 1984): 1, and Andersen, "Communication Ethics: The Non-Participant's Role," *Southern Speech Communication Journal* 49 (Spring 1984): 219–28.

7. Mary John Smith, *Persuasion and Human Action: A Review and Critique of Social Influence Theories* (Belmont, Calif.: Wadsworth, 1982), p. 5.

8. Richard Johannesen, "Perspectives on Ethics in Persuasion," in *Persuasion: Reception and Responsibility*, ed. Charles Larson (Belmont, Calif.: Wadsworth, 1986), p. 315.

9. Colin Turnbull, *The Mountain People* (New York: Simon & Schuster, 1972).

10. Peter Winch, "Nature and Convention," *Proceedings of the Aristotelian Society* 60 (1959–60): 242.

11. Ibid., p. 243.

12. Ibid., p. 244.

13. Ibid., p. 246.

14. Ibid.

15. Ibid.

16. Ibid., p. 249.

17. Ibid.

18. Ibid., p. 250.

19. Thonssen and Baird, p. 47.

20. Dag Hammarskjold, *Markings* (New York: Knopf, 1955), p. 112, cited in Nilsen, *Ethics of Speech Communication*, p. xi.

21. Bok, *Lying*, p. 31. Reprinted by permission of Pantheon Books, a division of Random House, Inc.

22. Nilsen, p. 46.

23. From Adrienne Rich, *On Lies, Secrets, and Silence: Selected Prose* (Norton, 1979), reprinted in Marilyn Pearsall, ed., *Women and Values* (Belmont, Calif.: Wadsworth, 1986), p. 353.

24. Ibid., p. 356.

25. Nilsen, p. 19.

26. Ibid., p. 14.

27. Sidney Jourard, *The Transparent Self* (Princeton, N.J.: Van Nostrand, 1964), p. 4.

28. Joe McGinniss, *The Selling of the President 1968* (New York: Pocket Books, 1970), pp. 82–83. Copyright © 1969 by Joemac Inc. Reprinted by permission of Simon & Schuster, Inc.

29. Although names have been changed to maintain anonymity, "A Question of Identity" is based on an actual story submitted by one of our students. We appreciate the willingness of the student to permit us to include the case in this text.

Chapter Four

1. Ernest Hemingway, *Death in the Afternoon* (New York: Scribners, 1932), p. 4. Cited in Marcus G. Singer, *Morals and Values* (New York: Scribners, 1977), p. 21.

2. Raymond Baumhart, *An Honest Profit: What Businessmen Say About Ethics in Business* (New York: Holt, Rinehart and Winston, 1968), pp. 11–12.

3. Sigmund Freud, *Civilization and Its Discontents*, trans. and ed. James Strachey (New York: Norton, 1961).

4. Lawrence Kohlberg, *Essays on Moral Development*, vol. 1 (San Francisco: Harper & Row, 1981).

5. Jean Piaget, *The Moral Judgment of the Child* (New York: Free Press, 1965).

6. For criticisms, see Margaret Donaldson, *Children's Minds* (London: Fontana/Croom Helm, 1978). Also see Martin Hoffman, "Empathy, Role-Taking, Guilt, and Development of Altruistic Motives," in *Moral Development and Behavior*, ed. Thomas Lickona (New York: Rinehart and Winston, 1976).

7. Lawrence Kohlberg, "Moral Stages and Socialization," *Essays on Moral Development*, vol. 2 (San Francisco: Harper & Row, 1983), p. 173.

8. *Sports Illustrated*, April 23, 1979, p. 126.

9. *Newsweek*, Aug. 6, 1979, p. 50.

10. Carol Gilligan, *In a Different Voice* (Cambridge: Harvard University Press, 1982). See also Kohlberg's reply to Gilligan in Lawrence Kohlberg, *Essays*, vol. 2.

11. For a good discussion of the relationship between justification and public advocacy, see Chapter 5 of Bernard Gert, *The Moral Rules* (New York: Harper & Row, 1970).

12. For more detailed treatments of the idea of universalizability, see, for example, Kurt Baier, *The Moral Point of View* (Ithaca: Cornell University Press, 1958), Chapter 8; and Marcus Singer, *Generalization in Ethics* (New York: Knopf, 1961), Chapter 2.

13. See Baier for a discussion of reversibility.

14. James Rachel's *Elements of Moral Philosophy* (New York: Random House, 1986) contains a helpful discussion of egoism.

15. For a classic statement of utilitarianism, see John Stuart Mill, *Utilitarianism* (New York: Liberal Arts Press, Bobbs-Merrill, 1957).

16. See, for example, Immanuel Kant, *Foundations of the Metaphysics of Morals* (New York: Liberal Arts Press, Bobbs-Merrill, 1959).

17. Roger Ricklefs, "Executives Apply Stiffer Standards Than Public to Ethical Dilemmas," *Wall Street Journal*, November 3, 1983.

18. Daniel Q. Haney, "Study Says Doctors Often Wrong on Patients' Wishes," *Kalamazoo Gazette*, April 29, 1984, p. C8.

Chapter Five

1. For a discussion of this distinction, see Margaret Carter, "The Morality of Deception" (Ph.D. diss., University of Wisconsin, 1982), Chapter 1.

2. Our colleague Joseph Ellin, Department of Philosophy, Western Michigan University (Kalamazoo), has suggested to us the following kind of exception. A known perjurer may lie, even though realizing that no one will believe the lie. It is not clear in what sense such a perjurer could be said to be intending to deceive.

3. Jeremy Bentham, *Principles of Morals and Legislation* (New York: Hefener, 1973), Chapter 16, section 24.

4. John Stuart Mill, *Utilitarianism* (New York: Liberal Arts Press, Bobbs-Merrill, 1957), p. 29.

5. Bok, *Lying*, pp. 32–33.

6. Carter, "The Morality of Deception."

7. See, for example, Immanuel Kant, *Foundations of the Metaphysics of Morals* (New York: Liberal Arts Press, Bobbs-Merrill, 1959).

8. This problem is discussed in Rita Manning, "Air Pollution: Group and Individual Obligations," *Environmental Ethics* (Fall 1984): 211–26.

9. Carter, p. 37. For support she cites Roderick Chisholm and Thomas Feehan, "The Intent to Deceive," *Journal of Philosophy* 74, no. 3 (March 1977): 153.

10. Charles Fried, *Right and Wrong* (Cambridge: Harvard University Press, 1978), p. 56. Cited in Carter, p. 38.

11. Fried, p. 57. Cited in Carter, p. 38.

12. Joseph Kupfer, "The Moral Presumption Against Lying," *Review of Metaphysics* 36 (September 1982): 103–26.

13. Ibid., p. 115

14. Ibid., p. 116.

15. Ibid., p. 118.

16. Ibid., p. 123.

17. Ibid., p. 124.

18. James Herriot, *All Creatures Great and Small* (New York: Bantam, 1973), pp. 298–302.

19. Jerry Green, "Rogers Packs Big Problem: Credibility," *Detroit News*, Feb. 7, 1985. Copyright 1985. Reprinted by permission of *The Detroit News*, a Gannett Newspaper.

20. Jay Mariotti, "Rogers: All I Want Is a Chance with Lions," *Detroit News*, Feb. 8, 1985. Copyright 1985. Reprinted by permission of *The Detroit News*, a Gannett Newspaper.

21. Mike Downey, *Detroit Free Press*, Feb. 8, 1985. Reprinted by permission of Mike Downey.

Chapter Six

1. Bok, *Lying*, Chapter 7, "Justification."

2. Frank Sibley, "The Rational and the Reasonable," *Philosophical Review* 62 (1953): 557.

3. John Rawls, *The Theory of Justice* (Cambridge, Mass.: Harvard University Press, 1971).

4. John Stuart Mill, "On Liberty," in *The Six Great Humanistic Essays of John Stuart Mill* (New York: Washington Square Press, 1963), pp. 52–53.

Chapter Seven

1. Irving Janis, *Groupthink*, 2nd ed. (Boston: Houghton Mifflin, 1982). Much of the discussion in this chapter is based on information in Janis's *Groupthink* and is used by permission of Houghton Mifflin Company.

2. *Group Dynamics: Groupthink*, July 1975. Reprinted by permission of McGraw-Hill Training Systems, P.O. Box 641, Del Mar, California 92014.

3. Ibid.

4. William C. Schutz, *The Interpersonal Underworld* (Palo Alto, Calif.: Science and Behavior Books, 1966).

5. Mill, "On Liberty," pp. 52–53.

Chapter Eight

1. Rogers Commission, "Report to the President by the Presidential Commission on the Space Shuttle Challenger Accident" (Washington, D.C., June 6, 1986), p. 40.

2. Ibid., p. 104.

3. "The Post-Apollo Space Program: Directions for the Future," "Space Task Force Group Report to the President," September 1969.

4. Rogers Commission, p. 2.

5. Ibid., p. 164.

6. Jim Heaphy, "Challenger's Trial of Blame," *In These Times* 8 (June 25–July 8): 3.

7. Heaphy and Rogers Commission.

8. See, for example, *Detroit Free Press*, June 11, 1986, p. 10A.

9. Rogers Commission, p. 165.

10. H. L. Nieburg, *In the Name of Science* (Chicago: Quadrangle Books, 1966).

11. Heaphy, p. 3.

12. "Back to Earth," *Nation*, Feb. 15, 1986, p. 164.

13. Rogers Commission, p. 148.

14. Ibid., p. 84.

15. William J. Broad, "Silence About Shuttle Flaw Attributed to Pitfalls of Pride," *New York Times*, Sept. 30, 1986, pp. 19, 21.

16. Ibid., p. 21.

17. Rogers Commission, p. 148.

18. Ibid., p. 93.

19. Howard Benedict, "Congress Plans to Watch NASA," *Detroit Free Press*, June 11, 1986, p. 4a.

20. Rogers Commission, p. 152.

21. Ibid., p. 153.

22. Ibid., p. 86.

23. Ibid., p. 92.

24. Dave Lindorff, "Engineers' Duty to Speak Out," *Nation*, June 28, 1986, p. 880. For a useful discussion regarding ethical issues in whistleblowing, see J. Vernon Jenson, "Ethical Tension Points in Whistleblowing." *Journal of Business Ethics* 6 (1987), pp. 321–328.

25. James C. Petersen and Dan Ferrell, Illinois Institute of Technology, Center for the Study of Ethics in the Professions: Module Series in Applied Ethics, *Whistleblowing: Ethical and Legal Issues in Expressing Dissent* (Dubuque, Iowa: Kendall Hunt, 1985).

26. Rogers Commission, p. 198.

27. Ibid., p. 103.

28. Everrett Rogers and Rekha Agarwala Rogers, *Communication in Organizations* (New York: Free Press, 1976).

29. Phillip Tompkins, "Management Qua Communication in Rocket Research and Development," *Communication Monographs* 44 (1977): 1–26.

30. Marshall B. Clinard and Peter C. Yeager, *Corporate Crime* (New York: Free Press, 1980), and Marshall B. Clinard, "Criminological Theories of Violations of Wartime Regulations," *American Sociological Review* 11 (June 1946): 258–70.

Chapter Nine

1. Much of the information in this chapter is from an interview with Jeb Stuart Magruder conducted by Studs Terkel and William Sloane Coffin. The complete text appears in Studs Terkel, "Reflections on a Course in Ethics: Jeb Stuart Magruder and a Question of Slippage," *Harper's*, October 1973, pp. 59–72. Copyright 1973 by Studs Terkel. Quotations are reprinted by permission of Candido Donadio & Associates.

2. Terkel, p. 59.

3. Terkel.

4. Jeb Stuart Magruder, *An American Life—One Man's Road to Watergate* (New York: Atheneum, 1974), pp. 378–79. Copyright © 1974 Jeb Stuart Magruder. Quotations are reprinted by permission of Atheneum Publishers, a division of Macmillan, Inc.

5. Ibid., p. 380.
6. Ibid.

Chapter Ten

1. *Detroit News*, June 4, 1986, p. SF.
2. Sissela Bok, *Secrets* (New York: Pantheon, 1982), Chapter 9.
3. See, for example, the debate between Monroe H. Freedman and Alan Goldman in *Criminal Justice Ethics*, Summer/Fall 1984, pp. 3–16.
4. *Nix* v. *Whiteside* (No. 84-13211), reported in the *New York Times*, Feb. 27, 1986, p. B11.
5. *Tarasoff* v. *the Regents of the University of California*, cited in Sissela Bok, *Secrets*, pp. 127–28.

INDEX